Mojo
Mom

Mojo Mom

Nurturing Your Self
While Raising a Family

AMY TIEMANN, PH.D.

GOTHAM BOOKS

GOTHAM BOOKS
Published by Penguin Group (USA) Inc.
375 Hudson Street, New York, New York 10014, U.S.A.
Penguin Group (Canada), 90 Eglinton Avenue East, Suite 700, Toronto, Ontario M4P 2Y3, Canada (a division
of Pearson Penguin Canada Inc.); Penguin Books Ltd, 80 Strand, London WC2R 0RL, England; Penguin
Ireland, 25 St Stephen's Green, Dublin 2, Ireland (a division of Penguin Books Ltd); Penguin Group (Australia),
250 Camberwell Road, Camberwell, Victoria 3124, Australia (a division of Pearson Australia Group Pty Ltd);
Penguin Books India Pvt Ltd, 11 Community Centre, Panchsheel Park, New Delhi—110 017, India; Penguin
Group (NZ), 67 Apollo Drive, Rosedale, North Shore 0632, New Zealand (a division of Pearson New Zealand
Ltd); Penguin Books (South Africa) (Pty) Ltd, 24 Sturdee Avenue, Rosebank, Johannesburg 2196, South Africa

Penguin Books Ltd, Registered Offices: 80 Strand, London WC2R 0RL, England

Published by Gotham Books, a member of Penguin Group (USA) Inc.

First printing, April 2009
10 9 8 7 6 5 4 3 2

Permissions are listed on page 227 and constitute an extension of the copyright page.

Gotham Books and the skyscraper logo are trademarks of Penguin Group (USA) Inc.

LIBRARY OF CONGRESS CATALOGING-IN-PUBLICATION DATA
Tiemann, Amy.
  Mojo mom: nurturing your self while raising a family / Amy Tiemann.
    p. cm.
  Includes bibliographical references.
  ISBN 978-1-592-40455-1
  1. Motherhood. 2. Mothers—Psychology. 3. Working mothers. I. Title.
  HQ759.T53 2009
  646.700885'2—dc22   2008053247

Printed in the United States of America
Set in Fairfield Light
Designed by Mia Risberg

While the author has made every effort to provide accurate telephone numbers and Internet addresses at the
time of publication, neither the publisher nor the author assumes any responsibility for errors, or for changes
that occur after publication. Further, the publisher does not have any control over and does not assume any
responsibility for author or third-party Web sites or their content.

This book is intended to be informational and should not be considered a substitute for advice from medical,
mental health, financial or legal professionals. The author and publisher assume no responsibilities for errors,
omissions, or inconsistencies herein.

Some names of Mojo Mom interviewees have been changed at their request.

"Mojo Mom" is a registered trademark of Spark Productions, LLC

To Ann, my Mojo Mom
And to my daughter,
who made this book possible
How can I ever say thank you?

Contents

Mojo Mom

The most important thing she'd learned over the years was that there was no way to be a perfect mother and a million ways to be a good one.

—JILL CHURCHILL, *Grime and Punishment*

What I did discuss, quite often rather unmercifully, was the impossible gap between the dream and the reality. I said that these were not super men and super women. These were people of ordinary quality . . . who were trying to do an impossible job.

—JOHN LE CARRÉ, master spy novelist, describing his work in a 1989 *Fresh Air* radio interview

What Is Mommy Mojo?

Mommy Mojo is the feeling you get when you are at the top of your game, juggling the many facets of your life and keeping your own needs in balance with family needs. It is the joyous feeling of becoming yourself and liking that person. It is the ability to speak, be heard, and make a difference in the world. It is power; it is being a force to be reckoned with. It is knowing that even if the rest of the world doesn't always realize how amazing you are, you can move through it like a secret agent, armed with the confidence that your plans will succeed on your own terms.

Today's new Moms were raised to believe that we could do anything. We are the daughters of *Free to Be . . . You and Me*, women who grew up assured that opportunity and equality were our birthright.

We have grown into accomplished women, armed with the skills to reach almost any professional goal. However, there is one major life transition that we have not been prepared for—motherhood. While there are hundreds of books that teach us how to care for a baby, there are very few that teach us how to navigate the monumental changes in identity that we face when we become mothers. Even the women who appear to have it all together may feel overwhelmed rather than overjoyed, leaving them to secretly wonder, *Who am I now that I am a Mom?*

The exciting news about becoming a mother is that it can feel like you are getting a brand-new life. And, like a Zen paradox, the bad news is . . . that it feels like you are getting a brand-new life. To make sense of this paradox, women often try to apply a career-ladder mentality to their evolving family relationships. This mind-set often leads to overinvolved parenting and sets women up to feel guilty and disappointed, because mothering does not pay off with tangible accomplishments that you can see and measure on a daily basis. While your work life may still operate according to a career ladder, your family life and mental landscape will shift.

If a career-ladder framework doesn't translate to motherhood, what does? I encourage you to view yourself as an artist. When you are an artist, no experience is ever wasted. Exploration and play are part of the process. Any connection or experience could stimulate a new insight that may prove valuable months or years from now. The artist metaphor can provide a useful alternative framework that frees us from the rigid roles that the world assigns us as mothers.

Mojo Mom will lead you on a path that starts with self-care, moves through creativity, and culminates in women's leadership. Motherhood is personal and political, and I firmly believe that addressing the unanswered questions about motherhood is our generational challenge. Feminism has pushed back the frontiers of gender discrimination by removing barriers to college entry and professional opportunities, but once women become mothers they may find that rigid gender roles snap into place with a vengeance—in their families, in their marriages, and at work. We will examine the full range of these issues, including the tension between what individual women can do and what needs to change in society. Lifelong career development will be a guiding theme, recognizing that there is no one-size-fits-all solution that will apply to every woman.

My own experience with the transition to motherhood motivated me to write *Mojo Mom*. My goal was to write the book I wished I had had when I was a new mother. When I was pregnant, I learned about the changes my body was going through as I grew a baby, and I learned how to care for a newborn. I didn't find much information about what was going to happen to me as a person. The advice I did find was always along the lines of "Take care of yourself because it will make you a better mother." This is certainly true, but it's not the whole story. Make no mistake about it: Mothers deserve to get their mojo back because they are worth it. Becoming a Mom does not mean that you have to sign away your rights to individual growth for the next twenty years. Each of us needs time, space, and support to meet our personal needs, in a way that is fair to everyone in the family. It can be done.

We all know that when we become mothers we receive a tremendous gift. I feel very privileged to have a child, and anything I say from here on is not meant to take away from that blessing. But I think many people would agree that the preparation most professional women receive for motherhood does not fit the true job description. This transition has always been hard to preview for a woman before she experiences it for herself, but we have to do a better job of telling the whole truth about motherhood. We have to be willing to look honestly at the challenges that we experience as mothers, as well as the gifts, in order to understand the full impact of this transformation on our lives.

What if there were another rite of passage in our society that often involved losing your job and professional status, even if it was temporary, changing your first name to "Mom," catapulting into a new social circle that required you to make many new friends, subjecting yourself to severe sleep deprivation, and suffering a loss of family income, in addition to becoming the primary caregiver of an infant? Does this sound like something that you would celebrate with a party featuring giant diaper-pin decorations and a ducky cake? It sounds more like an entry into the Witness Protection Program to me. It is certainly a challenge that requires new skills and survival strategies.

Even if we do physically return to the scenes of our old life, we can feel like alien visitors to a strange planet. For six years, as a graduate student at Stanford University, I strode across campus balancing a mocha latte in one hand and lab notebook in the other. I blended effortlessly into the crowd of students and professors that swarmed across White Plaza between classes. My work as a neuroscience graduate student had consumed me in an unhealthy way, and I knew that I was not going to stay on the research path that had been laid out for me, but for the moment at least, I felt like I belonged. Returning to campus a few years later, pushing my baby daughter in her stroller, I felt I no longer had any place in the campus community I had been part of for so long. I had finished my Ph.D. and had a successful teaching career under my belt, but my visit wasn't the triumphant return of Dr. Tiemann to Stanford—I was just an anonymous Mom looking for a pleasant stroller route.

No one consciously set out to make me feel invisible or inferior. But I no longer really knew who I was. My daughter was a wonderful and challenging baby. The transition from being a full-time teacher who planned two classes, gave five lectures, and interacted with hundreds of people a day to a stay-at-home Mom of a newborn who didn't sleep well completely threw me off my center.

To get to where I am today, I underwent a major phase of self-exploration and reinvention. In the beginning, I felt that my identity was stripped down to bare essentials. I was concerned only with getting through the day with enough food and sleep to do what I absolutely needed to do. This phase was not all bad. It gave me an opportunity to slow down and decide what was really important to me. When I had no more than a few minutes of time to myself, my priorities came into sharp focus.

As my brainpower and physical strength returned, I added new and old components into the mix: playing tennis to keep my body strong, making friends through a neighborhood Moms' group to establish roots in a new hometown. I reconnected with my dream of becoming a writer, and I found enough time and energy to finish a novel that had fallen by the wayside during my teaching years. I kept branching out, adding new skills, and taking advantage of opportunities that worked for my family and me. After my daughter started preschool, I felt my mojo rise as a surge of energy and creativity seeking an outlet. I experimented with teaching opportunities, improvisational comedy classes, and starting my own business. After a period of exploration and reflection, I focused on my love of writing and the ideas that became *Mojo Mom*. I knew that I was one of the best-supported women on the planet. I had a caring, supportive husband, a healthy child, financial security, and my own mother living nearby to help out. Even so, becoming a Mom was still the hardest thing I'd ever done. Once the reality of motherhood had sunk in, I realized there must be legions of other women out there who feel stressed out and overwhelmed by the challenges they face.

Isolation is a real problem for mothers. The good news is that, thanks to the power of online connections, no one needs to stay isolated for long. I created my Web site MojoMom.com to make it possible to have an ongoing conversation with my readers through my blog and *The Mojo Mom Podcast*. Of course real-world friendships are a crucial part of the equation, and on MojoMom.com I also offer a free Mojo Mom Party Kit to help you create your own gathering. Whether you are getting together a new group or meeting with old friends, a Mojo Mom's Night Out will help you get to know one another better as you are prompted to share stories about yourselves.

The Mojo Mom Party Kit contains several sessions so that you can meet once or form an ongoing group. You can try it out by hosting a party and seeing whether your group has chemistry. A group can be purely social—the book club without the book that many wish they had—or you can gather a group with a theme and goal. I formed an ongoing Mojo Advisory Circle two years ago, which has been one of the best things I have done for myself on both a personal and professional level. Our group of ten women meets monthly for networking, problem solving, and socializing. We are all mothers who either work on our own or are in business partnerships, and our Mojo Advisory Circle serves as our collaborative sounding board.

Here's my Mojo Mantra: Getting your mojo back is not just another item for your to-do list, but your *right*. All women need to continue to grow as individuals, not just as Moms. I will be the first to admit that having mojo is a recurring goal, not a permanent destination. I can feel competent, independent, and free one moment, then a few hours later feel I'm at the lowest point of mommyhood—when nothing is going right and everyone needs something from me. But the fact that I know I can get my mojo back again tomorrow helps me stay sane.

I wrote this book to help you get your mojo back and to show you that as mothers we're all in this together. Whether we talk about it openly or not, there are times when we all feel that we are at our wits' end. Being a Mojo Mom means being kind to yourself rather than feeling guilty when you are less than perfect, frustrated, overwhelmed, or just plain tired. This book is meant to help you find the time and space to continue developing your own identity, whether you're a new Mom for the first time, your kids are going to school and you have a little bit of time for yourself after many years, or you're reevaluating what you want to do with the rest of your life. Becoming comfortable with reinvention is a vital skill that will serve you well in many situations. Mothers whose kids have grown up and left home tell me that *Mojo Mom* takes on new meaning for them once they become empty nesters. Once you step over the threshold of motherhood, you'll find that you draw on your mojo reinvention skills at many milestones and transitions throughout life.

CHAPTER 1

A Mother Is Born

Sometimes you just have to take a leap
and build your wings on the way down.
—AUTHOR AND ENTREPRENEUR KOBI YAMADA

It is tempting to romanticize miraculous transformations. A homely, leaf-munching caterpillar spins a cocoon, goes through the process of metamorphosis, and emerges as a gorgeous butterfly. It's an image we're all familiar with, and we are always happy to see the new butterfly stretch her wings.

But I bet you have never asked yourself, *What about the caterpillar?*

When I was a brand-new mother, I focused on the fact that the caterpillar was gone.

When she entered the cocoon, she completely rearranged herself in order to reemerge as an amazing but different creature, one that is beautiful, strong, and able to soar to new heights. But one thing was for sure—she would never be a caterpillar again.

Becoming a Mom means that, like the caterpillar's life, your life will change in amazing, significant ways. It is a quantum leap rather than a gradual change. In one day your life will reorient itself, on physical, emotional, and practical levels. Getting a new life does not have to be a bad thing, but it comes as quite a shock if you don't realize that's what you are signing up to do. Our culture doesn't do a very good job of explaining this to people before they become parents. Birth is such a big event that it is natural that we overprepare for it, but we do new parents a disservice if we fail to look beyond the issues of delivery and infant care. In many ways, the birth industry is to motherhood as the wedding industry is to marriage. You get so caught up in the "big day" that you don't look beyond it to the rest of your life. A new baby is not just a temporary diversion in your plans, like a big project at work that takes over your life for a few months before things get back to normal. Adding children to your family means creating a new way of life. You will settle into a stable constellation—a new "normal"—but along the way you will be confronted by challenges you never imagined.

The changes in identity that come along with the transition to motherhood are rarely previewed to women before they have children. After the baby arrives, it is jarring to realize that other people's perceptions of you have suddenly, radically changed. You give birth, and just when you feel ready to go back to your old self, you realize you have stepped into a new role that society has defined for you. Laura, a nonprofit agency director, describes her experience this way:

> I was totally unprepared for the way the loss of personal identity that comes from being a mother would affect me in the beginning. Just a few weeks after my son was born, I celebrated my thirty-seventh birthday. My family was great, and gathered together at our place. I was still nursing all the time, and wasn't feeling very well as I recovered slowly from the C-section birth that happened after a twenty-hour labor. I remember being disappointed and confused when all of the presents and cards revolved around the baby—baby clothes, baby pictures, cards that said,

"Happy Birthday, Mommy!" I also felt guilty for not thinking this was okay—shouldn't I embrace my new identity? Why would I expect to be the focus when there was this beautiful, amazing, and demanding creature attached to me all the time?

Laura's sense of dislocation echoes the theme of *Mojo Mom*: Who am I now that I am a Mom? We will spend the rest of the book exploring this question, celebrating the discoveries that come along with this journey while looking honestly at motherhood's challenges and losses.

Becoming a parent sets you on a lifelong path of constantly evolving challenges. By the time you've figured out the terrible twos, you are faced with new three-year-old issues. Having a baby means that five years from now you'll be the parent of a kindergartner, and in thirteen years you'll have a teenager! You are signing up for challenges you cannot even imagine yet.

The clash between expectation and reality can be one of the most stressful aspects of the initiation into motherhood, especially for women who are used to being in control of most aspects of their lives.

Motherhood is an exercise in letting go of absolute control and making peace with chaos. One of my goals is to give women a more realistic view of what motherhood is really like, to ease the transition of becoming a Mom. The early weeks of motherhood can come as a shock to your system. Whether you stay at home or go back to work after a short leave, the postpartum period can seem otherworldly, as your body recovers, your emotions swing from one end of the spectrum to the other, and you adjust to your new role and become comfortable mothering your baby. You are faced with the paradox that on the one hand, newborns really don't do anything other than eat and sleep, but on the other hand, infant care and household duties can literally take up your whole day. You may have reacted quizzically if you have heard other new Moms talk about how they didn't even have time to take a shower—wondering, *How is that even possible, and will it apply to me?* Then, after you bring your own little one home, you see how the household mess piles up and other maintenance tasks fall by the wayside while you devote your time to your baby. How are you going to cook when you don't even have time to load last night's dishes into the dishwasher? It's a great gift to have an involved partner or others to take over the housework while you get your bearings, but no matter how much help you have, you will feel tired. My newborn daughter wanted to be carried at all times, and she howled with anger from six to eight P.M. each evening if I didn't rock her in an awkward "Superman" hold, laying her across my forearms as though she were flying. It was exhausting, but the alternative—hearing her cry inconsolably—was unbearable to me. She was born a little early, and her nervous system seemed immature and irritable. She outgrew that after a couple of months, but for the first eight weeks or so, I paid the price as my sleep debt and physical exhaustion mounted. I felt like we should have performed a ground-touching ceremony for her when she was forty days old, like they have in Asia, because it felt like she barely spent any time out of Mommy's or Daddy's arms until then. No wonder the rest of my world felt like it had temporarily ceased to exist.

Why is our modern American preparation for motherhood so unrealistic? First, girls are no longer automatically expected to participate in household tasks and care for younger siblings the way they used to be. Many first-time Moms have never seen a newborn up close or taken care of a baby before. This may be the first time a career woman has assumed the responsibilities of full-time caregiving—and believe me, when you spend your day at home with a new baby, housework increases exponentially. As soon as one mess has been cleaned up, another one pops up somewhere else. The days of leaving at seven

A.M. and coming home at seven P.M. to a house that has stayed exactly the same are over.

While each of us grapples with the elusive question of what it means to be "a good mother," we may worry about the job we are doing when our personal experience contradicts our fantasy ideals. There are days that we'll feel ambivalent, resentful, or depressed. Despite our best efforts, we may feel like our family views us as servants, that our accomplishments are unappreciated and our identity erased. Sheer exhaustion and sleep deprivation may cause us to feel disconnected from our better selves. As unpleasant as these feelings may be, they are normal. We each deserve a chance to process and express our emotions through a safe, trustworthy outlet, whether that's a friend, family member, support group, or counselor. The alternative—hiding behind an inauthentic "mask of motherhood," and seeing other Moms wearing it—can leave us feeling isolated, ashamed, and insecure. When women do admit these feelings, they are often surprised and relieved to hear that other Moms feel the same way. It is time to gather the courage to take off our masks and allow ourselves to look honestly at all aspects of motherhood. Doing so will pave the way for us to claim our authentic lives and will help all women to choose motherhood based on a more realistic idea of the commitments they are making.

The expressive taboos of the mask extend to our society's lack of realistic parenting education, which tends to either begin at conception and end at birth, or focus on the baby's needs in minute detail without much consideration of the parents. You could fill a bookshelf with encyclopedic pregnancy and child-care volumes that barely address the changes in parents' lives and the identity transformations that accompany motherhood.

Finally, we are so inundated by mythical images of idealized motherhood that we are most likely unaware of their impact on us. We are literally being sold an unrealistic image of motherhood as we are bombarded by consumer pitches to sell us the newest gadget that promises to make our lives more relaxing, enriched, and organic, all at the same time. After the baby arrives, romanticized pregnancy advertisements give way to subtle suggestions that we can buy our way to becoming a better mother if only we'd shell out for the latest safety device or child-enrichment toy. We are dazzled by articles showing us how quickly celebrities like Jennifer Lopez lose their baby weight and

Don't Call Me "Mom"

One of my pet peeves is that in many situations, adults simply call a mother "Mom" without even bothering to find out her name. This typically occurs in places like the pediatrician's office, where a nurse or doctor will say, "Okay, Mom, please help Mackenzie up onto the table so that I can examine her." I understand that this is a shortcut for health-care professionals who see dozens of people a day, but it still always bugs me to be referred to so generically. Sometimes even people who know a woman's name still address her as "Mom" when her children are present. Again, this is an understandable choice, but one that gets under my skin. My daughter will still know who I am if she hears me called "Amy."

The irony is that in writing *Mojo Mom*, I am faced with calling my readers "Mom" throughout the book. I wish I could address the book personally to each of you! In recognition of the fact that "Mom" takes place of our individual names in so many situations in life, I have chosen to capitalize "Mom" and "Dad" throughout the book, while "mother" and "father" remain lowercase.

become "yummy mummies"—putting pressure on the rest of us to do the same, even though we don't have personal trainers, around-the-clock nannies, and chefs at our disposal. Celebrity magazines are obsessed with "baby bumps," and you half expect these famous offspring to pop out of the womb bearing a cell phone preprogrammed to call their publicist. While celebrity Moms are usually working parents, we hear over and over again that stars like Jodie Foster and Celine Dion have fabulously successful careers, yet claim that they would much rather be home with the kids if they really had their way. If an Oscar-winning actress wishes she had my life, who am I to complain? (Douglas and Michaels, *The Mommy Myth*, p. 136).

✳ Honoring Your Caterpillar Self

Becoming a mother takes on a new set of challenges when a woman has spent thirty years or more developing into the most wonderful caterpillar she could be before becoming a butterfly. The older a woman is when she becomes a Mom, the more of her established identity she has to leave behind. However, the good news is that when you stay connected to your essential self, you can decide which aspects of your old life and identity you do want to carry forward, or rekindle in a new way. It *is* possible to recognize and honor parts of your "caterpillar self" in your new "butterfly life."

Our generation's specific identity crisis is a sequel to Betty Friedan's *Feminine Mystique* and her articulation of "the problem that has no name." In the 1950s and into the 1960s, if a woman was privileged enough to attend college, she was typically there in pursuit of a "Mrs." degree, or living in married housing as a "Ph.T." wife, working while "Putting Husband Through" college as an investment in both of their futures. A woman was often expected to move directly from her father's home to establish her husband's household, without ever living on her own outside of a dorm or sorority. If she took on a job, it was assumed to be a temporary diversion until she fulfilled her destiny as a mother. Once she had children, her family became her sole focus. Her own personal growth was put aside, and she was expected to live vicariously through the accomplishments of her husband and children. As we know now, many of these housewives felt empty inside and saw their marriages crumble, often decades later, after the social landscape had shifted. Susan, a mother of two who married in 1969, just after college graduation, and divorced in 1989, said that the restrictive roles assigned to her in marriage made her feel like "I was a bird in a cage, and I handed my husband the key."

As women demanded more than a secondhand identity, the women's movement of the 1970s was born. The next generation of daughters was raised to feel that they could work alongside men as equals and accomplish anything. These girls grew up with *Free to Be . . . You and Me*, the Bionic Woman, and Princess Leia. Their role models included female astronauts and political leaders. They excelled in high school and went on to college and graduate school to get B.A.'s, M.F.A.'s, J.D.'s, and Ph.D.'s. After years spent building independent lives and successful careers, they took the plunge into motherhood and had kids of their own.

So here we are, at the fragile juncture between feminism and reality, which defaults more toward the 1950s version of family life than we ever could have imagined. Motherhood brings gender roles to the forefront, and many of us are shocked to find how quickly our paths diverge from those that our husbands and other male peers are following. This doesn't mean that we have to follow the stereotypically feminine, domesticated path, but it does mean that we are likely to feel the pressures to head home, starting with the fact that our modern workforce is still based on an assumption that workers are men with stay-at-home wives who take care of family duties. Even women who appear to have made different "choices" may in fact be respond-ing differently to the same pressures: From day one we are presented with totally inadequate family-leave policies and typically unsupport-ive bosses. Many mothers are not able to exercise their personal pref-erences for continuing their careers on their own timelines because of the lack of public policy and company policies that support maternity leave and a return to work.

Sociologist Pamela Stone conducted research to find out what was really going on behind the phenomenon that others had called "The Opt-Out Revolution." Stone found that male bosses consistently applauded women who left their jobs for "making the right decision" to quit, rather than finding a solution that would allow them to con-tinue working. Women reported that employers were willing to throw money at them to stay full-time but were not willing to entertain the idea of part-time work. While we certainly want at-home Moms to feel supported, so should employed Moms. We deserve more options than a black-and-white "choice" to stay—working as though nothing has changed—or go home.

On the marriage front, Stone found that even a formerly egalitar-ian husband may choose the male path of wanting to "step on the gas" to advance his career, as he feels increased pressure to be a breadwin-ner, leading his wife to "hit the brakes" once the baby arrives. She is likely to feel the pressure to stay home, be the one to adopt a flexible career, or take on the responsibilities of finding and managing paid child care when she goes back to work.

Becoming a Mojo Mom is about making individual choices and finding the path that works for each of us, but it is important to re-main aware that our choices take place in a context that still does not support working mothers the way it should. Child rearing is an essential part of life and society, but all too often this work is expected to remain invisible and undervalued. Mothers should be allowed to work, and fathers should be allowed to parent, without having their employers question their ability or loyalty if they take advantage of parental leave or need to miss a day of work to care for a sick child. I believe that an overdue revolution in work is on the way, one in which results will mean more than face time, and flexible work options such as telecommuting will become standard.

The three generations currently in the workforce may eventually find common ground on the benefits of truly flexible work, as Boomer bosses decide they want phased retirement, busy Gen X parents need to balance work and family, and Millennial twentysomethings burst onto the scene wondering why the workplace would ever operate any other way. However, it remains to be seen whether this wave of change will arrive in time to help the current generation of new parents. Even in the midst of frustration, it may give us courage to recognize that we can be pioneers on the front lines of change.

For now, it is still challenging to integrate our families and our careers. We are left with an overloaded balancing act if we choose to resume our careers, or a life that may not be at all as we imagined if we stay home with our children. On top of it all, somewhere in this complicated equation, we hope that we can find a place for *ourselves* in our lives.

Mojo is not really a new concept, but it is one that every generation of women has to reinvent for itself. We've come through the feminine mystique and the second and third waves of feminism, and yet motherhood still feels like the forefront of a revolution in everything from personal identity to social policy.

My fervent hope is that in twenty-first-century America, women can feel free to talk honestly about the joys of motherhood and the fact that some days being a Mom can be a lonely and stifling existence; that it is okay for mothers to save some of their best time, energy, and creativity for themselves; and that their partners and children will

support them in this effort by creating family structures that allow Mom to get her mojo back.

✳ Mojo Activities

The caterpillar-cocoon-butterfly transition is the image that best de-scribes my experience, but no single metaphor can express the variety of changes that come along with motherhood. Create your own meta-phor of your transformation into a mother. Share your metaphor with a friend and ask her how she would describe her experience.

Older mothers have a great deal of insight into the process of reclaiming their mojo. Ask your mother or another supportive woman of her generation what it felt like to become a mother. She will have the benefit of many years of perspective, knowing how her identity changed as her children grew up. It is fascinating to explore the sim-ilarities and differences in the experiences of women who became mothers before and after the start of the second-wave feminist move-ment of the 1960s and 70s.

If you are feeling a loss of your old self, it can be helpful to give yourself permission to mourn the loss of your old life before mother-hood (your caterpillar self). Find a way to express these feelings, and honorably say good-bye to the parts of your old life you may not be able to—or don't want to—reclaim. Find a trusted friend who will listen to your losses without minimizing them. Once you have let go of the idea of returning to life just as it was before you became a mother, you will have more emotional energy to devote to finding new pathways in your life.

It may be helpful to create a ritual or take an action that symbol-izes this transition. Something as simple as throwing out old files or textbooks that correspond to a career that is no longer your passion, or donating clothes that no longer suit your style, even if they fit you, can help make room for new interests.

If there is a part of your caterpillar self that you have put aside but long to reclaim, keep reading. We will revisit this challenge in Chapter 3, "Banking the Embers of Your Self . . . to Build a Bonfire Later." You may be able to revive that part of your life, or you can identify its essence and come up with a new outlet that gives you the same feeling.

REFERENCES AND RESOURCES

The Feminine Mystique by Betty Friedan

First published in 1963, Friedan's revolutionary work has been called "the book that pulled the trigger on history" and ignited the second wave of the feminist movement.

The Mask of Motherhood: How Becoming a Mother Changes Our Lives and Why We Never Talk About It by Susan Maushart

Maushart examines the unspoken cultural pressures and taboos that prevent mothers from expressing their full range of feelings, and the psychological and social implications of wearing the inauthentic mask of motherhood.

The Mommy Myth: The Idealization of Motherhood and How It Has Undermined Women by Susan Douglas and Meredith Michaels

Douglas and Michaels make a compelling case for the damage done by the "cult of new momism"—the modern American vision of motherhood that sets unrealistic, romanticized standards of perfection that are forever out of reach.

The 7 Stages of Motherhood: Making the Most of Your Life as a Mom by Ann Pleshette Murphy

Pleshette Murphy's guide previews the seismic shifts that mothers undergo at each stage of their children's development, from birth through the teen years, giving you a preview of the road you'll be traveling.

Our generation's challenge is to get mothers' concerns addressed on a political and policy level. For a look at recent developments in feminism and politics, I recommend:

The F-Word: Feminism in Jeopardy—Women, Politics, and the Future by Kristin Rowe-Finkbeiner

Sisterhood, Interrupted: From Radical Women to Grrls Gone Wild by Deborah Siegel

Full Frontal Feminism: A Young Woman's Guide to Why Feminism Matters by Jessica Valenti

CHAPTER 2

Life Inside the Cocoon: The Early Months of Motherhood

The days are long but the years are short.
—MOM'S WISDOM

A *note to seasoned Moms: We've all been through those early days of motherhood. In this chapter, we need to get our new mojo sisters caught up on basic survival skills. Join us to relive those first months of motherhood, or meet us in the next chapter, where we will explore ways to make sure that we include ourselves in our list of priorities.*

My neighbor is eight and a half months pregnant with her first child. Seeing her walk by, the inevitable waddle taking over her stride, her bulging belly balancing awkwardly on her small frame, I can remember the feeling I had in the last weeks of pregnancy: *Just let me put this baby down and everything will be easier.*

Pregnancy is a marathon. No matter how excited you are about having a baby, sharing your body with another person for nine months inevitably leads to periods of grumpiness. You barely recognize the form your body has taken, and you haven't even seen significant parts of yourself, such as your feet, for weeks. It seems as if everything you eat gives you heartburn, you can't find a comfortable sleeping position, and even if you do fall asleep, you have to get up three times a night to pee anyway.

By the end, the baby may seem like a roommate who eats the last scoop of ice cream you were saving, steals your favorite pillow, and parties all night while you try to sleep.

You think, *Bring on the birth, and just let me put this baby down!*

Then, a miracle occurs. The baby is born. Women's birth experiences and their feelings about them are incredibly diverse. Birth can be the most empowering experience in a woman's life; it can feel like a well-managed, smooth transition; or it can be very scary if complications arise for the mother or baby, or if the woman feels unsupported by her delivery team. I urge you to share your birth experience with other Moms, and get support for any unresolved feelings.

A new little stranger enters your life and expands your family. Every woman experiences a unique moment in which she realizes that she really is a Mom. My moment came when my midwife asked for "Mom's birth date" for the birth record, and I started to say "1942" before I realized she was talking about *my* birth date, not my mother's. *I* was suddenly "Mom," and my own mother was promoted to "Grannie Annie."

You may feel from day one that you've known your baby forever, or it may take a while to develop a bond. Either way is okay. Poet Adrienne Rich reminds us that for many women "motherhood is earned, first through an intense physical and psychological rite of passage— pregnancy and childbirth—then through learning to nurture, which does not come by instinct" (Rich, *Of Woman Born*, p. 12). Depending on your birth experience and your physical, hormonal, and emotional condition, you may not feel a connection with your baby right away. Please don't burden yourself with an extra helping of guilt if this is the case. You've finally put the baby down, but your work has just begun. To survive and thrive as a Mom, you will need to be very, very kind to yourself.

> *You really have to love yourself to get*
> *anything done in this world.*
> —LUCILLE BALL

Your recovering body is the first indication that life as you know it has really changed. No matter how comfortable you were with your body before or during pregnancy, after giving birth your body may suddenly feel like a foreign land, with rough terrain and no road map. In my experience talking to lots of mothers, postpartum recovery is likely to be a phase that no one has really prepared them for. After a vaginal birth, your private parts can be so swollen and bruised that they may feel as if they've been turned inside out. If you are one of the approximately 30 percent of American women who give birth via Cesarean section, you face recovery from abdominal surgery in addition to the other physical challenges of birth. After either birth method, you will bleed as though you have a heavy period for several weeks (payback for nine months without one?). Your belly may feel like bread dough that has just been punched down after rising. You can't sit up without propping yourself up on your elbows because your abdominal muscles are too stretched out to contract. The good news is that recovery does occur, and relatively quickly for most women, considering what their bodies were just asked to do. The bad news is that all of those "old lady" ailments you've laughed at up to this point start creeping into your life: Hemorrhoids, varicose veins, and bunions may be here to stay.

In an ideal world, a new mother would receive as much care and pampering as her baby, but unfortunately our culture frequently does a terrible job of mothering the mother after birth. I grew up hearing stories about my own birth, but never connected my own mother's experience with the fact that I was going to have to solve that puzzle for myself one day. My mother gave birth to me in the Naval Hospital on the remote Pacific island of Guam. Three days later, when a typhoon was approaching, she had to get up to iron my Dad's shirts so that he could work an extended shift at his job at the hospital, leaving Mom home alone with me. I don't know which aspect of this story bothers me most—that she had to fend for herself with a newborn during a typhoon, that my Dad expected her to iron his shirts, or that she did it! Now that I am a mother and understand all that she did on her own, her strength astounds me. She had no child-care experience, and there she was living thousands of miles away from her family and friends on a military assignment. She learned the ropes on her own, cradling me in one hand and holding her "instruction manual"—*Dr. Spock's Baby and Childcare*—in the other. Thank you, Mom, and thank you, Dr. Spock. For all of *Baby and Childcare*'s imperfections, it gave her a foundation that fostered her confidence in herself. She quickly grew into a wonderful mother.

When I asked my Mom how she survived with so little help, she was her usual stoic self: "I didn't even know help was something I could ask for, and if I had asked for it, I don't know whether I would have gotten it." Life doesn't have to be this way. It shouldn't be. In many cultures around the world it would be unthinkable to leave a Mom and newborn alone together for hours every day. But in modern American culture, new parents frequently live far away from the close family and friends who could provide the support they need. It is crucial to create as much support for a new Mom as possible. Help could come in the form of Dad taking paternity leave, inviting in relatives to provide care, reaching out to friends for support, or hiring someone to help with housecleaning, cooking, and babysitting older children.

Sybil, the mother of three children ages seven and younger, offers this advice:

A good friend, pregnant with twins, called me one day with questions about hiring help. When to have it? Day? Night? Just a few hours? For a few weeks? She was so confused and overwhelmed, and asked if I could somehow simplify it for her. I paused for a moment, reflecting on my experiences with my newborn babies, and then I replied, "Yes, I can simplify it for you: Get as much help as you can reasonably afford." We laughed because it seemed so funny and ridiculous, but I explained why I thought it also had truth to it. A few months after her twins were born, she said our conversation that day really opened her eyes. They had brought on as much help as they could, and she felt it had saved her sanity. She was so grateful that I had been willing to be honest with her.

Medically speaking, the postpartum period extends about six weeks after delivery and eight to twelve weeks after a C-section, but you may not feel back to normal yet at that time, especially when you factor in the physicality and sleep deprivation that come with parenting a newborn. Ideally, a new Mom needs several weeks of pure nesting; a time when she can focus her energies on getting to know her baby, breastfeeding, if she chooses to do so, and her own rest and physical recovery. She may choose to be up and about, taking a stroller walk or a trip to the grocery store, but it's nice if she doesn't have to. This is no time to be Superwoman! The magical, dreamy weeks after birth are a time of rest and recovery from one of the biggest physical and emotional changes you will ever experience. When you are caring for yourself and a newborn, it is time to let go as much as possible, for as long as you can.

Life inside the cocoon is an intense time. Motherhood is truly a marathon, not a sprint, and the first eight to twelve weeks are particularly all-consuming. You will find your way back to the world and develop your own personal parenting style, but in the beginning, as you deal with the demands of a newborn and adjust to your new life, you need only to focus on moving forward one day at a time, doing whatever it takes for you to feel sane.

Not all women have the luxury of choosing an extended nesting period. Women with older children to care for, single Moms, or mothers who return to work within a few days or weeks after birth have an even greater need for a ready, willing, and able support network. It can be really difficult to ask for help, but I urge you to do so. If this is your first baby, you may feel eager to prove that you can do it all and "be the Mom." I was somewhat defensive about getting advice and help with my newborn because I thought it meant that I wasn't able to do it on my own. I kept telling my mother, "I am a capable and competent person." The phrase became a running joke after a while. Looking back now, here's what I'd say to my new Mom self: Relax. You will do it all, and then some. You are going to be a Mom for the rest of your life, and you will raise this child with your husband and family, not to mention the whole world of your friends, your child's friends and their parents, as well as the neighbors, doctors, and teachers who will enter the picture. Though you may feel as territorial and protective as a mama bear with a new cub, I urge you to take advantage of all the help you can get. Let your partner be as involved as possible. Enjoy watching Daddy bond with Baby.

There Are Many Ways to Get Help

Here is the number one recommendation from my readers: If you have family nearby, be grateful for that resource and find a way to incorporate them into your lives. Even if you have full-time child care, family support is always valuable, on a personal and practical level. Child-care gaps inevitably arise for sick days or school holidays, and it's a gift to have someone who is willing to step in at a moment's notice.

Consider hiring a doula or other postpartum support professional to help you get off to a good start, as well as a babysitter to help care for older children, if necessary.

Research breastfeeding support options and new parents' classes in your area before you have your baby. You don't necessarily need to have delivered your baby at a given hospital to take advantage of their postpartum services.

Find affordable and nutritious meal take-out or delivery options near you.

Accept offers of help from friends when the new baby arrives.

Hire a cleaning service at home if you can afford it.

Over time, develop a roster of babysitters you trust.

Make friends with other families in your neighborhood. Offer to help them, and ask for help when you need it.

Set up a babysitting co-op among friends (see www.BabysittingCoop.com) or a rotating weekly family supper club.

Find a friend who will work on home-improvement projects, organizing, or cleaning with you.

Make new friends at work. There may be other supportive Moms to meet if you seek them out.

Network through online communities, while taking steps to protect your family's privacy along the way. Be conscious about what family or personal information you are making public.

A good therapist or counselor can be a vital resource. Think about whom you'd go to if a crisis arose. If you encounter a major life crisis, don't feel that you have to fix it on your own. Reach out for help.

If you practice a religion, take advantage of the nursery service at your house of worship to get a weekly break for prayer and meditation. It may be your most peaceful hour of the week!

Worship communities may also sponsor Moms' support groups, playgroups, or preschool classes. These preschools are often preferentially available to members, so get information about the application process well before you need it.

Of course, when you receive unsupportive, unsolicited advice—which you will at some point—you will need to decide when to advocate for your views and when to let criticism roll off your back. It is important to stand up to family members or authority figures, such as doctors or parenting experts, who undermine your confidence in your own parenting style by imposing their views upon you. As you sort through all the advice, you will become an advocate for your evolving parenting style. Pick your battles carefully. You will get all sorts of contradictory comments from friends and strangers: You're dressing the baby too warmly or not warmly enough; you are feeding the baby too much or too little. When this happens, I recommend you check that the baby is okay, then put on your most serene smile and say nothing, or simply say, "Thank you for your concern," before moving on. This is one time that a mask can serve as a protective shield. Debating every piece of advice you receive will just wear you out.

Newborn babies are strange little individuals. First of all, if you've never seen one up close before, be prepared: They don't look anything like the newborns you see on TV, who are played by six-month-old baby actors. Newborns tend to look like aliens—cute aliens, but aliens nonetheless. They have large eyes and broad foreheads. Their skin can look too large for their body, sagging in strange folds, and can quickly become peppered with baby acne and flaky cradle cap. Their heads may be pointy or oddly shaped from being squeezed during birth. And their bodies can be strangely proportioned, from having big hands or ears that the rest of the body needs to grow into, to having temporarily enlarged genitals from normal exposure to maternal hormones. Every baby is unique and cute in its own way, but if the baby looks really different than you expected, you can feel a little disappointed at first. Don't panic. Your baby will fill out and look less like an alien and more like the Gerber baby within a few months.

On to our next newborn reality check: Babies come equipped with a variety of sleep styles, and unfortunately, you can't custom order one! Your baby's ever-evolving sleep style will have a big impact on how much rest you are able to get. Remember that you are in this for the long haul. Even if you feel pretty jazzed and energized at week two, changes in your baby's schedule or your own cumulative sleep deprivation may turn you into a walking zombie in a few months. I saw this in myself when I watched the weekly videos we made after our daughter was born. From weeks six to ten, I became visibly more and more tired. My eyes glazed over and I sounded very dreamy when I talked. I was really happy to be a Mom, but I was wholly unprepared for the feeling of losing my intellect (even temporarily) and existing in an otherworldly state of consciousness. This is why continued self-care is so important.

Depending on how agreeable your baby's natural sleep habits are, you may spend a lot of time reading sleep-advice books. If you are a first-time Mom, you may not yet realize that sleep is one of the most heated battlegrounds among parenting experts. There is a wide spectrum of advice available, from the "gradually let them cry it out" camp of Dr. Richard Ferber to the "wear your baby and share the family bed" position of Dr. William Sears and the attachment-parenting movement. Arguments about what really works can become polarized and heated among parents as well. There will always be someone who claims that there's only one way to solve a baby's sleep problems, and you may feel a lot of pressure to conform to one style or another. I recommend *The Sleep Book for Tired Parents* by Becky Huntley as a refreshingly balanced resource. It cuts through the debates, covering all four of the basic sleep approaches—family bed, cry it out, teaching in small steps, and living with it—without favoring one over another.

I am convinced that if you have the confidence to trust your own instincts, any one of several alternatives can work out fine. By trusting your intuition, you won't let yourself subscribe to a system that harms your baby or your family. Read a variety of parenting advice books, even some you think you won't agree with. This will expose you to a range of opinions about child rearing, illuminating the fact that there is no one right way to parent. Try a method, and if it feels wrong or stops working, adapt the method to fit your needs or try something else. Many issues, such as the quest for a good night's sleep, end up being ongoing processes that evolve as your child develops, rather than battles to be conquered once. Our family shared the bed for nine months before we decided we needed our daughter to sleep in her crib. We followed a lot of attachment-parenting ideas at first, which were nice for my baby but tough on me. My back ached from carrying her in her sling, having her fall asleep in my arms, then being unable to transfer her to a crib. I lay down next to her in bed for every nap, except for the occasional times that she fell asleep in a bouncy chair or car seat. It was great at first, but after a few months, I craved time on my own to do something other than nap or read. After all that time being pregnant and wanting to put the baby down, I felt I didn't really put her down for quite a while! If I had the opportunity to do it all again with a second child, I would put a high priority on getting the baby to sleep day and night in a crib within a few months. For all the debate about co-sleeping, the most important thing to remember is that the family bed has to work for the whole family. There has been growing discussion about "reluctant co-sleepers," parents who don't want their kids to sleep with them but have not developed an alternative routine, so the kids end up with them, or the parents end up sleeping with the kids in their beds (Green, "Whose Bed Is It, Anyway?"). After you make it past the early months of nighttime feedings, the best sleep routine is whatever it takes to get a good night's sleep for everyone, including Mom and Dad. It is worth working through short-term struggles to achieve long-term peace.

Parent trainer Donna Erickson gave me one of the best pieces of advice I've received, wisdom that applies to many parenting situations: "What is familiar is preferred." In so many parenting challenges, Mom and Dad will need to persevere to transform a new activity into a familiar routine. If you are willing to stick with it and overcome your baby's initial resistance, you can teach your baby to accept routines that work for all members of the family. In some cases we have no choice: All babies must ride in car seats whether they like it or not, and they eventually get used to it. The same principle can apply to sleeping in a crib.

I am a bit of a crusader about sleep issues because I have lived with the consequences of chronic sleep deprivation, and nothing else works as well as it should if you are not well rested. Yes, the early weeks and months are something of a struggle, but after that my watchword is "sustainability." We talk about sustainability as a strategy for the environment, and the truth is that sustainability starts at home with family life. As a mother, you are creating relationships and habits that could last a lifetime for you and your child. You might be able to get away with poor sleep habits for weeks or months—at a cost—but to stay happy and healthy over the long run, it is vitally important to develop a parenting style that nurtures your needs as well as your family's.

With that in mind, there are three important questions to ask yourself about any parenting advice you receive:

1. Does the advice meet my standards of common sense?
2. Does the recommendation match my family's value system?
3. Is this approach sustainable in the long run?

Do not let any parenting expert pressure you into adopting a parenting style that is unsustainable for you. Maternal burnout is a real danger that can have serious consequences for your health and well-being and that of your family.

Your own parenting style will evolve by trial and error over time, including the changes that come with additional children. Listen to the advice of trusted friends and experts, decide what works for you, and don't be afraid to try something new when you run into challenges. Mothers have always had to figure out the balance between listening to expert advice and figuring things out one day at a time. Betsy, one of the women in my Mojo Advisory Circle, shared her family's story about her grandmother's challenge with a new baby decades ago:

When my aunt was days old, very colicky and screaming up a storm, my grandmother consulted a book. On one page it said, "The baby with colic is underfed"—so my grandmother fed her—no luck. She went back to the book—on the next page it said, "The baby with colic is overfed." At this my grandmother threw up her arms. When she shared the story with my wise grandfather, he said, "Well, you have two choices: you can either throw the book out the window, or the baby." With that, my grandmother tossed that book out the window. The baby is seventy years old today.

Getting Support for Postpartum Depression

While postpartum depression (PPD) is not inevitable, up to half of new Moms experience it, most commonly six to eight weeks after giving birth. Some of the symptoms of postpartum depression, such as feeling like a failure, or having weird, uncontrollable thoughts or crying spells, can be embarrassing to admit. Other symptoms can include anxiety, phobias, feelings of hopelessness, loss of concentration, loss of appetite, or sleep disturbances (insomnia or hypersomnia).

The most powerful words you can say to your family or doctor are "I'm not doing well and I need help." This conversation may be easier if you decide in advance whom you can talk to about what you are going through. PPD can occur after your first baby, or after the third or fourth. Family members and friends should keep an eye out for signs of PPD and offer help if they are concerned. It is important to talk to your doctor if you think you may be experiencing PPD, because certain physical illnesses or hormonal imbalances can masquerade as PPD. Sleep deprivation can be a complicating factor as well, since all new parents are overtired and sleep becomes a precious commodity. Your doctor can direct you to appropriate treatment and therapy, and identify support groups in your community.

This Isn't What I Expected by Karen Kleiman and Valerie Raskin is a comprehensive guide to recognizing PPD and getting help. Kleiman and Raskin observe that:

> *In our practices, we discovered that some women who suffer from depression after childbirth recognize it right*

away; others suffer alone, knowing that they feel miserable but not aware that postpartum depression is a real illness, with a name and a cure. We have yet to see a woman suffering from postpartum depression who expected it—we have all grown up expecting that this would be one of the best times of our lives. (p. xi)

Please don't suffer in silence. Help is out there—ask for it.

Rejoining "The World"

You will reintegrate yourself into the world according to your own schedule. Some women, especially seasoned Moms with other children to care for, quickly return to their daily routines. Others realize one day that it's time to take down the Christmas decorations because it's July Fourth. In either case, once you are ready to venture outside your cocoon, it's time to meet other Moms. This is especially important if you are going to stay at home with your baby for an extended period of time. Even if you are a fiercely independent woman who has not socialized much in the past, I highly recommend that you get plugged in to a network of mothers. They will provide a support system and safety net and can save your sanity when you need it most. I can promise you with near certainty that there will be times, due to accident, illness, traffic, weather, or other unforeseen events, that you will have to call another Mom to ask her to drop what she is doing to take care of your child. This is true whether you are partnered or single, staying at home or employed. Even with my own mother living in my neighborhood, I have had to do this myself.

One night when my husband was out of town, I became sick at ten P.M. and had to ask a neighbor to come stay with my sleeping toddler while my Mom drove me to the emergency room. In addition to emergencies, your network can help lighten the burden of everyday scheduled inconveniences. Believe me, it is more comfortable to go to the gynecologist without an inquisitive toddler in tow! Best of all, friendships are forged out of the web of mutual dependence we weave with other families.

What about your old friends? As much as you value them and want to stay in touch, the reality is that it is a challenge to maintain friendships that are built around work or child-free socialization after you become a Mom. Your life and schedule are now radically different, and even if you return to work, you may not feel like "one of the gang" anymore—though you may find new friends and allies at work whom you didn't know before. In the office and out, your days of carefree socializing will be replaced by intense scheduling and juggling. If you are blessed with close friends without children who stick with you through the transition to parenthood, great. They will most likely be true friends who have made a real commitment to being in your life. In any case, it will be essential to develop a core group of friends who are also Moms, preferably including a few who have more experience than you do. You can hook up with other new Moms in several ways. In addition to informal neighborhood networking, many cities have organized Moms' clubs or other groups, such as La Leche League, that bring mothers together. Online socializing for Moms has developed in many forms, from virtual networking to organizing in-person Meetup groups.

I highly recommend taking a New Mom or New Parent class—with your partner, if possible—if you can find a good class in your area. Many hospitals offer an ongoing series of classes as community outreach, and you can often take classes at the nearest hospital even if you did not deliver your baby there. In addition to being a great way to meet new Moms with babies the same age as yours, having access to live expert advice is priceless. When my six-week-old began projectile vomiting every day, I worriedly scanned my stack of baby books and came up with a possible explanation of "pyloric stenosis," a condition that "could easily be corrected with a simple surgery." Needless to say, that was not very reassuring! Thankfully, I could turn to my New Mom class teacher Donna Erickson during our weekly meetings. She

Sex After the Baby Arrives

Part of rediscovering your body after giving birth will be reconnecting with your sexuality and your partner. It can be intimidating to imagine getting back into sex, but the good news is that your body *can* recover.

Many women conveniently forget to mention to their partners when their doctor has told them that it is physically safe to resume intercourse. Your doctor's permission is not a mandate—you don't need to give your partner the green light until you are ready. Healing can take a while, especially if you had a perineal tear. As always, talk to your health-care provider if you have questions or concerns.

When you do feel ready, it helps to have a relaxing setting, but don't go overboard to create a big date night that has unrealistically high expectations. My idea of a romantic setting for this event would be any location where your baby is not in the next room!

Ease back into sex with touching and exploration. If you get around to intercourse, great. If you try intercourse and it is too uncomfortable, stop and try it again another time. You can find other ways to bring each other to orgasm if you wish.

If you haven't discovered the wonders of lubrication yet, this is the time to try a slick, slippery lubricant such as Astroglide, which is available at most drugstores. Look for a lubricant with propylene glycol as a major ingredient. I recommend a thin liquid that requires only a few drops, not any sort of gummy, gooey jelly.

The mental and physical aspects of lovemaking are equally important. Examine your beliefs and possible fears about resuming physical intimacy. I discovered that I had a deeply ingrained, almost subconscious assumption that sex could never possibly feel good again after giving birth. This is one time that I am happy to report that I was *wrong*!

correctly assessed that I was simply feeding the baby too much each time she nursed, causing her to spit up. The problem was so mundane that it didn't make it into any of the books I consulted, but it was a real crisis for our family, and one that we needed help solving. (If you are wondering why I couldn't figure this out on my own, it was because I was so concerned about making *enough* breast milk that I never considered that I might be producing *more* than my baby needed at each feeding.)

Outside of organized gatherings, informal Mom networking occurs all over the place. Finding new friends can be both fun and stressful, sort of like dating all over again—but this time you are looking for a different kind of soul mate. If you are working full-time, it can be tough to make these connections because many Moms' groups meet during the day. Many working Moms report that it is worth it to make networking a priority, even if you have to do even more juggling to fit it into your schedule.

Katherine, who has cemented many friendships through motherhood, explains the connection among Moms this way:

Our playgroup was a godsend for me. When I had Jackson, I had no friends with children. It was so nice to find a group of women who understood my situation with no explanation necessary. Becoming a Mom is like getting an invitation to a secret society. You suddenly have so much in common with strangers. It's a really neat feeling! I find myself starting conversations in the checkout line or in a restaurant with another Mom and having so much to talk about, just because we are both Moms.

Katherine found out just how strong her network of friends was when she was pregnant with her second child. At twenty-six weeks of gestation, Katherine began to experience preterm labor and had to be hospitalized to stabilize her pregnancy. She spent two months in the hospital and she experienced several more scary moments, but she was able to hold off delivery until she reached thirty-two and a half weeks. During Katherine's two-month hospital stay, she never spent a night alone. Her friends showed up to stay with her, and helped her husband and son back home as well. The fact that Katherine had made these close friendships before she reached a crisis meant that when a crisis hit, her whole neighborhood sprang into action to help the family. Her daughter Sawyer is now a happy, healthy five-year-old, and Katherine says that while her hospitalization was an intense time full of genuine worries, looking back, it now seems like a distant memory. Her life has gone back to normal in a good way, and she says she will never move away from her neighborhood because she knows how lucky she is to be part of a close-knit group of Moms.

Keep searching for women you connect with, and don't give up until you've gathered a handful of good Mom friends. They will be by your side for years to come.

❈ Going Back to Work

Going back to work is naturally accompanied by mixed feelings. Even if you are fortunate enough to have adequate parental leave (which few families have in the United States), when the day comes to return to work, you may feel happy to be returning to the adult world and work role you are so familiar with, but also sad to leave your child in someone else's care. As a mother, you may feel pulled in a million different directions, especially during the first days back, when you may not be feeling totally recovered from the postpartum period yet.

Just about every industrialized country except the United States has a national policy that covers paid family leave. We lag far behind the rest of the world in this area. Families in the United States are left to cobble together their own parental leave plans using disability insurance, accrued sick days, and vacation leave, if their employer does not choose to provide paid leave. The Family and Medical Leave Act (FMLA) grants some workers twelve weeks of unpaid leave, but that law covers only about six in ten workers in the private sector. In some companies, even when parental leave or flexible work options are offered, individual bosses or the corporate culture may stigmatize these options as career suicide. Additionally, it's one thing to be entitled to unpaid leave and another to be able to afford to take it. On the policy and corporate levels, our incomplete, patchwork system of coverage leaves families scrambling for a work–family–child-care solution.

Given our current system, mothers are left doing the best they can to put together their maternity leave and back-to-work transition plans. Holly is the mother of a two-year-old daughter and an eight-month-old son. She has held the position of director of an MBA program for working professionals for five years. Her job is intense at times, requiring evening and weekend work, but she appreciates that her position has enough flexibility built in that she is able to see her kids and run errands on days that are not as heavily scheduled.

After each of her children was born, Holly pooled together her sick leave and vacation leave to get twelve weeks of paid leave. She felt fortunate that she had been at her job long enough to save up the time to craft this paid time at home. If she had been new at her job, she would have had to settle for unpaid leave or returned to work sooner. During each maternity leave, Holly spent about two weeks away from her office with no communication, while another university staffer took over her day-to-day role. After those first two weeks, Holly began to get back in touch with her office through phone calls and e-mail, ramping her way back up to working four to twenty hours a week at home, on her own time. From home, she could work her way through a stack of student applications to evaluate, and participate in "interview blitz" conference calls with her colleagues. Technology was her lifeline to stay in touch and get back up to speed before returning to work full-time.

Holly wishes her university, which is one of the state's largest employers, offered more generous and comprehensive parental leave policies, but she also feels grateful that her immediate supervisors have a favorable attitude toward flexibility, allowing her to continue working over the long run while she raises her two children.

A Working Mother's Wish List

As Mojo Mom, I have worked with a wide variety of mothers' groups, and I am proud that both employed Moms and stay-at-home Moms have been interested in my ideas. I wanted to get more information about what helps women make the transition back to work, so I sent a questionnaire to my MojoMom.com readers asking about the kinds of support at work and home that they relied on, or wished they had available to them. I received responses from forty-two employed mothers and compared them with detailed responses from thirteen women who identified themselves as stay-at-home mothers. Together these responses create a comprehensive list of the factors that help these Moms make it all happen on a daily basis. There was a great deal of common ground in that all mothers feel busy and stressed at times, and it's a challenge to find time to for self-care. In addition, employed mothers faced specific workplace issues in addition to managing and enjoying family life. Here are some of the top factors that mothers were concerned about as they returned to their paid jobs:

Child care is a top priority, and it is clearly a challenge to find affordable, quality placements. Families come up with all sorts of solutions, from traditional day care to nannies to family home care. You can never have too many backup resources, whether they be additional babysitters, friends, or family. The mothers I surveyed either deeply appreciated family members who could help out in a pinch or wished they had that resource available.

Bosses can make all the difference. No matter what a company's official policy states, your individual boss's attitude matters. An understanding, supportive boss is a godsend. A rigid, clueless, or just plain mean boss can make life at work difficult. Even employers who claim to be supportive can miss the point. Karen, a grants manager and mother of two, had this experience after returning to her job after an eight-week leave:

> *I will still never forget after I was struggling to stay awake in a meeting soon after coming back to work, my boss saw this and sent me to HR, where the HR person suggested I was "being too hard on myself." But if it had been up to me, I wouldn't have been at that meeting in the first place! I needed fewer re-*

sponsibilities and less work during that time, but my leave was over. They were not flexible at all with respect to part-time work. Then having my difficulties attributed to my being too hard on myself, as opposed to their expectations, just seemed like blaming the victim all over again.

I ultimately left that job a couple of years later, over those kinds of flexibility issues. My current employer has a different attitude toward flexibility, which makes a difference.

The initial transition back to work will always be a challenge. Many of the women I surveyed recommended coming back to work midweek, if possible, to troubleshoot the first few days and then rest up over the weekend, rather than facing a solid five days by returning on a Monday. Between navigating child-care logistics, finding a starting point for your projects, and adjusting to mothers-only challenges such as pumping breast milk at work, there is always a lot going on during this time.

Once you are back on the job, be on the lookout for new allies. There may be other mothers at work that you have not known up to this point who can serve as valuable sounding boards. The unique book *The Milk Memos* developed from a notebook that a group of nursing Moms working at IBM left in their "pumping palace"—a converted janitor's closet in the ladies' restroom, a far-from-luxurious accommodation, but ultimately a space that they made their own. They formed an extended sisterhood through the messages each woman wrote to the others as she sat alone, pumping milk. They welcomed new "Milk Mamas" as more coworkers became mothers, and the group developed a deep pool of collective wisdom to help one another make it through a challenging time. They advised each new mother to set a "reevaluate date" well into the future, giving herself a chance to really adjust to her new situation before deciding whether it was really working for her. The Milk Mamas say, "Don't race for the exit door yet. The emotions you feel in the first few weeks are raw and can lead you to believe that working motherhood is miserable or impossible. It's not! Give yourself a couple of months before making any big decisions—about your job, breastfeeding, or moving to the sticks and living the 'simple life'" (Colburn-Smith and Serrette, *The Milk Memos*, p. 24).

At home, a partner's hands-on involvement is a powerful sustaining resource. Your new parenting partnership may take time to develop, and no matter how long you have known each other, and even if you already have kids together, your relationship will remain an evolving work in progress. Kristin, a biologist whose children are eighteen, five, and four-year-old twins, shares her personal story of relationship renegotiation:

> *Men are more able to help than they are willing to admit. I needed physical help with getting the busywork of keeping a home accomplished. When I got a job offer too good to resist, I went back to work on a part-time basis. While my husband made limited attempts to hold everything together in my absence, a huge pile of work was left for me when I returned. That just made me feel resentful and I frequently rode around the house on a broomstick. After a few "Come to Jesus" moments, he put forth a Herculean effort to try and take my place while I was gone for work. I am happy to report that he is now marvelous at being me.*

Working Moms are always going to be pulled in multiple directions. The changes in focus can be a blessing as well as a hazard. One mother pointed out that "most professional working mothers admit that they like being back at work and prefer it to being home. It is a return to 'normal' for them after the jolt a baby brings. Going to work every day is almost a relief from the chaos, but in exchange the so-called balancing act begins to run her life."

A career can be fulfilling in many ways, but a working mother can also feel that her sense of personal identity gets pushed off the stage as she scrambles to make sure her boss's needs and family's needs are met. Amanda, a sociologist who now has three kids, describes her experience this way:

For me, motherhood represented a huge identity crisis. I spent most of those early parenting years working as a full-time graduate student with a loving husband who traveled full-time for a living. I was exhausted most of the time and there was so much to be done all the time that I found myself organizing my time around the care and satisfaction of others.

I completely lost myself in the process of bouncing back and forth between the desire to please everyone at home and everyone at work. It all culminated in what could best be described as a panic attack one afternoon when I realized that I was coming apart at the seams. I didn't actually know what I wanted anymore. I don't mean that I wanted to quit motherhood or my graduate program, but something much more insidious than that. I was completely panicked at the thought that I couldn't make everyone happy all the time anymore. I was completely strung out in terms of exhaustion and overwork, and I didn't know myself anymore. I had no opinion anymore about what to eat for dinner or who to vote for in the next election.

To make matters worse, my body image was drastically shaken by the weight gain, and unfortunate lack of loss, associated with pregnancy. I no longer had the free time to make the kinds of food I liked, to read the kinds of books I liked, or watch television or listen to the radio. I didn't even have the time to exercise each day—the one thing that could keep the stress at bay and give me a few minutes of solitary reflection.

Amanda made it through this difficult time by figuring out what her must-have support activities were, and finding a way to do them, no matter what. She decided that exercise was necessary, even though "I couldn't make the gym work (my babies apparently screamed too much in the nursery) so I looked like a crazy mother hauling my kids around a multi-mile trail circuit in some combination of jog strollers and backpacks."

Taken collectively, the responses I received from more than fifty mothers created a remarkable degree of consensus about the personal support lifelines that are essential for all Moms. I asked, "What is the most important thing you do for yourself?" The responses coalesced around *basic physical needs*, including sleep, good food, and exercise; *mental needs* for some time alone to think, read, or meditate; and *social needs*, including time to play with their kids without worrying about work, as well as adult time spent with their partners, or socializing with friends. When there was no free time to be found, many mothers reported that they would get up early each morning, before the rest of the family, to carve out time for their essential self-care activities.

We will talk more about setting and realizing your personal priorities as we head into the next chapter.

☀ Mojo Activities

Take gentle care of yourself during the fragile months following birth. It is helpful to start preparing for this time before the baby arrives, but be prepared to modify your plan once you meet your unique baby. Sit down with your partner or family and draw up a list of resources you can turn to for help. Consider the resources and assistance that family, friends, community, and paid help can provide. In the early months, help with household chores, cooking and cleaning, and care for older siblings can be extremely helpful. It's never too early to start looking for good child care or babysitters, even if you don't think you will need these services right away.

If there are gaps in your support system, work together to find ways to get the assistance you need. This may require you to extend your budget to invest in paid assistance, or you can extend yourself within your personal network by asking for help, as well as offering help to other families. While this can feel awkward at first, the good news is that connecting with other parents and friends in this way can grow long-lasting friendships.

Don't be afraid to tell your partner what you need. Families are not mind readers, and it is much healthier—and more effective!—to ask for what we need rather than stew in silence and resentment because we aren't getting enough participation from the rest of the family. When you do ask family members for help, you'll need to be prepared to be specific in your requests. Try to encourage and appreciate your family's efforts even when the results fall short of what you would do yourself. It's a good time to adopt the mantra "*Done* is better than *perfect*."

↝ REFERENCES AND RESOURCES

Mothering the New Mother: Women's Feelings and Needs After Childbirth by Sally Placksin

This La Leche League publication is a well-written support and resource guide for new Moms during the first year after birth.

I Wish Someone Had Told Me: A Realistic Guide to Early Motherhood by Nina Barrett

Barrett takes an unflinching look at the physical, emotional, and social challenges that women face in the first months of motherhood. She debunks common mothering myths, giving women an honest look at the realities of this transition.

This Isn't What I Expected: Overcoming Post-Partum Depression by Karen R. Kleiman and Valerie Davis Raskin

This comprehensive guide details the symptoms of postpartum depression and describes a self-help program for women to use alone or with a therapist. It also provides information about mobilizing support from your husband or partner, family, and friends.

The Sleep Book for Tired Parents: Help for Solving Children's Sleep Problems by Becky Huntley

This workbook equally considers four different sleep philosophies, helps you decide which approach is the best fit for your family, and tells you how to implement it. I recommend reading this before and after the baby arrives.

The Milk Memos: How Real Moms Learned to Mix Business with Babies—and How You Can, Too by Cate Colburn-Smith and Andrea Serrette

The Milk Mamas provide helpful practical advice as well as inspiration and empathy. This is an essential guide for mothers who continue breastfeeding while working.

This Is How We Do It: The Working Mothers' Manifesto by Carol Evans

The Working Mother's Guide to Life: Strategies, Secrets, and Solutions by Linda Mason

Carol Evans is the CEO and president of *Working Mother* magazine, and Linda Mason is the cofounder of Bright Horizons Family Solutions child care. These two women are truly experts on helping working mothers create successful work and family lives.

The Stay-at-Home Mom Survival Guide: Field-Tested Strategies for Staying Smart, Sane, and Connected While Caring for Your Kids by Melissa Stanton

From making Mom friends to creating daily routines, Stanton gets into the nuts-and-bolts, practical issues of creating an enjoyable experience as a stay-at-home Mom.

CHAPTER 3

Banking the Embers of Your Self . . . to Build a Bonfire Later

A single event can awaken within us a stranger totally unknown to us. To be alive is to be slowly born.

—ANTOINE DE SAINT-EXUPÉRY

As you emerge from the cocoon of the early postpartum period, it is time to start getting to know your new self. This may feel like a time of flux, when you decide which parts of your old life can be carried over or adapted to fit your new life as a parent. This period may be accompanied by feelings of exhilaration, pride, exhaustion, confusion, being overwhelmed—or all of the above. The Chinese character for "crisis"—which some have interpreted as a combination of elements signifying danger and opportunity—is an appropriate symbol for this juncture. The danger is the possibility of losing your way, your connection with who you are, and what you need. At the same time, the opportunity to reinvent oneself can be a precious gift, one that offers freedom to make radical changes. You may reshape a career that was not satisfying you, examine your priorities, start a new venture, or rekindle long-dormant interests. Many people (men in particular) never feel the freedom and opportunity to reinvent themselves in this way, but the transition to motherhood virtually guarantees that you will reevaluate your core self. Choices that you once took for granted you will now make consciously, and obligations that were once easily fulfilled will now be completed with much greater effort.

It is likely that the decision to go back to work or to stay at home will be a significant one. You may find that the plan you had originally counted on does not feel right anymore. Perhaps you thought you would work but now want to stay at home, or vice versa. The aim of *Mojo Mom* is not to convince you that one path is better than

The Challenges and Gifts of Motherhood

As Compiled by the Chapel Hill Mojo Sisters

This list will always be a work in progress. How is your own experience similar or different?

Challenges

Constancy of never-ending responsibility
Endless work with little to show for it on a daily basis
Little recognition or praise for mothering as compared
to the positive feedback you get from a professional
career

Having no time for yourself

Sleep deprivation

Depression

Balancing professional life and family life

Body-image issues during the first year after birth, struggling to lose the pregnancy weight

Having less confidence

Dealing with so much change all at once

Ending or changing your career

Having to go back to work and be at the top of your game, even when you are exhausted

Mothering a sick child at home and having no downtime to recoup your energy

Worrying about what others think

Moving to a new home or town

The isolation of staying at home

Day-care sickness and the resulting gaps in child care

Guilt over working or guilt over not working

Feeling guilty or feeling like less of a mother for not breastfeeding

Feeling overwhelmed by the gap between expectation and reality

Feeling the pressure to keep it all together

Not having time to exercise

Antidotes to the Challenges

Honesty

Confidence

Partner support

Letting go of control, having realistic expectations, working

together with your partner, buying in to your new life
as a parent

Finding validation wherever you can

Playgroups—connecting with other women can be a
lifesaver

Remembering your old self, creating a new self, and being
willing to change

Dressing up—don't get stuck wearing grungy clothes all
day

Starting a new venture—a business or a class

Exercising and taking care of your health

Your priorities come into focus, making you more attentive
to the things that are truly important; no more wasting
time on things or people that aren't

The Gifts of Motherhood

The gifts of motherhood can be harder to quantify and explain than
the challenges. Joan McIntosh expresses this conundrum perfectly
when she says, "It is easy to complain about children. But when we
want to express our joy, our love, the words elude us. Our feelings
are almost so sacred they defy speech." Here are some thoughts to
start a list that each of us must complete for ourselves:

Allowing your children to show you what is truly important
in life

As a parent, connecting and empathizing with the world in
a new and meaningful way

Stepping out of the rat race and enjoying simple moments

Feeling part of the continuation of life

Relearning the joy of kid's play

Experiencing the feeling of receiving by giving

Becoming comfortable with the fact that you are an adult

Experiencing the senses that engrave memories: the smell of a newborn's fuzzy head, the feeling of your child's hand holding yours, the sound of a preschooler lost in giggles, the tears that stream down your face as you watch your child's graduation

The wonderful feeling of being in love

In the best times, the ordinary will transcend the mundane, and becoming a parent may help you connect with William Blake's profound wish:

> *To see a World in a Grain of Sand*
> *And Heaven in a Wild Flower*
> *Hold Infinity in the palm of your hand*
> *And Eternity in an hour*
> —Auguries of Innocence

the other, but rather to encourage you to honestly examine what your needs are as a person and a family, and to craft a plan that works. The process I've created to help you design your new life assumes that every new mother goes through similar stages in sequence—at her own pace—whether these stages are carried out at home, at work, or both.

The Four Phases of Getting Your Mojo Back

The chronology of the Mojo Mom plan generally follows the process of a Mom re-creating her identity after having her first child. The plan has four phases: (1) survival mode, (2) incubating your desires, (3) setting priorities and goals, and (4) taking baby steps toward your goals. These ideas can be adapted for Moms of any age and number of children by retraining the family to make Mom's needs a priority, and enlisting the help of your partner, family and friends, and other trusted caregivers as necessary and appropriate. Each woman will spend as much time as she needs in each phase. Don't judge what you need by other women's timing.

Phase One: Survival Mode

During survival mode, you are still in the early weeks of motherhood described in Chapter 2. Be gentle and generous with yourself during this period of settling in, recovering physically and emotionally, and getting to know your new baby—or babies, since about 3.5 percent of pregnancies are multiples. Enjoy the positive aspects of life inside the cocoon and remember that your baby will grow beyond this sometimes-unsettled newborn stage. If you plan to return to work soon after your baby is born, make sure you arrange as much help as you can to ensure your rest and recovery while meeting your baby's needs. Getting outside assistance will help you conserve your energy for the things only you can do. Last time I checked, it was still impossible to hire someone to sleep for you, so it is perfectly legitimate to ask for help with housework and child care so that you can take a nap. Making your self-care a priority from day one will create healthy habits that will help you avoid burnout down the road. This isn't selfishness; it's self-preservation. Happy parents are the foundation of happy families.

Phase Two: Incubating Your Desires

Your desire to pursue your interests may return before you can arrange to pursue them, leading to a period that feels uncomfortable and restrictive. Rather than fighting this restlessness, you can explore it to find out *what you really do want to do*. Marilyn Paul was writing about getting organized when she shared this wisdom, but it can be applied directly to a Mom's process of incubating her desires:

> *As you observe and write, you will get a clearer sense of your current reality; you'll notice that there is probably quite a gap between what you have now and what you want. Author Robert Fritz says this is the essence of the creative process. According to him, part of the work that artists do is holding the gap between where they are and what they want. As they hold the gap and take the actions that will bring their creative vision into reality, they often feel a great deal of creative tension. (Paul,* It's Hard to Make a Difference When You Can't Find Your Keys, *pp. 72–73)*

You can use this tension to propel your creative self forward. Ask yourself what you would want to do if you had the free time. What would you do with two hours, a free afternoon, or a day on your own? Which of these can you realistically arrange? If your baby is a good napper, you may be able to devote a couple of hours to yourself on a regular basis. The trick is to use your available time to do something you enjoy, not just to clean the bathroom! Make sure that your partner understands that having time to yourself is important, even if you just get away to browse in your favorite bookstore, take a walk by yourself, or connect with friends at a Moms' night out. This is not wasted time, but a precious opportunity to recharge your batteries and maintain your interests and strong relationships with your friends. Of course, couple time is also extremely important, and we'll discuss that in detail in Chapter 7, "Daddies as Mojo Partners."

All parents need downtime, whether they are employed or staying at home. It can feel difficult, awkward, or unfair to ask for this time, though it is essential to do so. Laura, whom we heard from in Chapter 1, was employed while her husband cared for their son:

> *While I'm glad that we made the choice that we did, I think that it's been harder for me to take any guilt-free time for myself because my husband is staying at home. At work, I feel I have to make sure I maximize my time and get as much done as possible. At home, my son clings to me during most waking moments, and my husband is wiped out from his long day of child care. I love spending time with my son, but the trade-off seems to be pursuing personal interests such as reading, cooking, spending time with friends who don't have kids, or just getting something done around the house.*

You can learn to appreciate any opportunity to catch a little time to yourself. For me, one of the great lessons of motherhood is that I almost never feel bored when I am on my own. When you are watching over your child, even if he or she is sound asleep in another room, there is a powerful sense of Mom vigilance that is always humming in the back of your mind. This powerful survival tool is an amazing gift and skill. However, it is draining to have your subconscious radar turned on twenty-four hours a day, every day, which is why I advocate the absolute necessity of having some time to yourself when you are relieved of child-care duties.

The freedom to be lost in my own thoughts, even in the most mundane situation, has become something to be valued, not dreaded. After struggling to entertain a restless three-year-old on a long airplane trip, making the same trip by myself became a luxurious chunk of free time. Other parents have told me that the commute home, an airport layover, or even waiting alone in a doctor's office can be appreciated as a welcome respite from the constant barrage of questions and demands coming from their families. These breaks come along naturally during the course of the day; the key is to notice and savor them. I look at college students spending entire afternoons studying at a coffeehouse and think back to how little I appreciated the freedom of being a full-time student. Now I get it!

Phase Three: Setting Priorities and Goals

Once you have cultivated your desires, you will begin to act on them. When your mojo begins to reawaken, your first desires might not seem productive or related to your ultimate goals. The key is to notice that your energy and attention are coming back. Feel that energy, play with it, and then redirect it in a productive way. Looking back, I see that one of the first indications that I was getting my mojo back was that I started spending time on eBay buying movie memorabilia. It was a strange thing to be doing, but it was at least a sign that I had some time and inclination to redevelop my personal interests. I wrote a novel and screenplay before writing *Mojo Mom*, so the movie angle did give me a clue that pointed me toward my renewed passion for writing.

Your eventual goal is to become a master at setting your priorities and sticking to them by protecting and spending your time wisely.

When your children get older, the demands on your time from school, the community, or your kids' activities will become even more numerous. There may always be thirty-six hours of demands on your twenty-four-hour day, and you will have to learn to say no to many of those demands in order to get the essentials done—and to stay sane. This is hard for many women because saying no is one of the biggest causes of Mom guilt. Many of us have been socialized to be people pleasers who will do everything asked of us. This caretaking tendency often intensifies after having children. It is vitally important to learn the skill of saying no. Setting boundaries that exclude nonessential activities will truly create more time and space to say yes to things that are enjoyable and meaningful.

Gateway to Your To-Do List

> *The art of being wise is the art of knowing what to overlook.*
> —WILLIAM JAMES

I have three criteria to apply to any item trying to make its way onto my to-do list: *Is the activity fun, meaningful, or absolutely necessary?* If it is none of these, the demand can be respectfully declined or let go without any guilt or explanation other than "I won't be able to take that on right now." Resist the temptation to apologize or overexplain your reasons for saying no. Any discussion beyond that point is an attempt by someone to try to get you to change your mind. Remember that you are not doing anyone a favor by taking on a responsibility that you are ill-equipped to manage.

For activities that are fun, meaningful, or absolutely necessary, you must still strike a balance because there will invariably be too much to do.

As you schedule your priorities, make sure that you include eating, sleeping, exercise, and regular medical care
for yourself as essential needs that are nonnegotiable.

This may sound obvious to the point of being ridiculous, but too
many mothers neglect their basic needs and feel chronically unwell
and depleted. When my daughter was a toddler, I was struggling
on the edge of chronic exhaustion, so my doctor recommended an
overnight sleep observation in a neurology lab to get tested for sleep
disorders and screened for depression. After extensive testing, the
doctor's expert diagnosis was "You need to sleep more." Two years
of cumulative sleep debt had taken its toll, and I was prescribed
a nine-thirty P.M. bedtime for the next six months. There was no
shortcut to get around the fact that I had to make up that deficit, so
I did, even though it was difficult to give up precious hours of free
time I had enjoyed at night after my daughter went to sleep. Once
I caught up with my body's needs, I felt like myself again, without
needing any additional treatment or medication. I just wish I had
allowed myself to make sleep a priority without needing a doctor to
prescribe it for me.

For tasks that are absolutely necessary but not fun or meaningful,
you have several options. You can:

- Choose to do it yourself anyway (inevitable sometimes, but
  not recommended)
- Get someone else to do it by
    - delegating the task to a family member
    - sharing the task with a friend
    - hiring outside help
- Change the task in a way that makes it more fun or meaningful
- Reevaluate the demand and decide it is not absolutely neces-
  sary after all

Do all members of your family participate in housework? *Being a Mom is signing up for a life of service, but not life as everyone's servant.* All family members need to share responsibility for household chores, an arrangement that each family uniquely negotiates. You need to stay on top of the arrangements the family agrees to, and adapt them as necessary. A mother's feeling of being overwhelmed and underappreciated is a toxic combination that will fester into resentment if it continues over time. It is essential that the family does not allow this to happen. Teach your children to do what they can for themselves. Even preschoolers can work alongside you with a dust rag, sponge, kid-size broom, or damp paper towel. Don't worry whether the little ones are doing a good job; just get them involved. Instead of buying your children toy appliances, why not buy them real tools? Montessori school equipment suppliers sell functional child-size versions of many cooking, cleaning, and woodworking tools. My favorite source is www.ForSmallHands.com.

Letting go of a task is a valid option. You may as well start practicing it now, because there is always more work to be done than one person or family can humanly accomplish. Mojo Mom Laura, the nonprofit director, learned a more balanced approach from her husband:

> It seems to me that most women are socialized to think that they should do everything at home; the whole "Martha Stewart" phenomenon makes things worse. I have never been particularly competent in the domestic sphere, and my husband of ten years has always done most of the cooking. What I admire about him as a stay-at-home Dad is that he doesn't agonize about the things that he can't get done. It doesn't really matter in the long run if the house is a mess, but it does matter if our son gets lots of positive attention. It doesn't really matter if the mountains of photographs don't make it into albums for a few years; if we have

food on the table to eat dinner together, that's enough. It has been important for me to let go of my unrealistic expectations of what it means to have a stay-at-home parent (of either gender) and just learn to go with the flow.

One of the Mojo Activities for this chapter is to make a list of the major obligations you have, and to rate each one as fun, meaningful, or absolutely necessary. Which obligations can you cross off or get someone else to do? Which can you enhance with extra meaning or fun? The point is not to add tons of exotic new activities to your list, but to reach a healthy level of obligation and scheduling, and to find ways to enjoy what you already do.

As you go through this process, think carefully about which fun, meaningful, or important activities represent your truest values and priorities. When I taught high school, my students were bright over-achievers who wanted to do everything, and they tended to be hor-ribly overscheduled. My science teacher colleagues and I used to ask our students to imagine the classic management scenario involving rocks, pebbles, and sand in order to think about how they set their priorities.

Imagine an empty gallon-size glass jar. Your job is to fill it with a mixture of rocks, pebbles, and sand. What happens if you fill the jar to the top with golf-ball-size rocks? Is there still space left? Yes. There is room for you to pour in smaller pebbles. Is the jar completely full now? Not yet. There is still some space left between the pebbles and rocks. If you poured sand in, you would completely fill the jar.

The rocks are your high-priority tasks and goals, pebbles are aver-age priorities, and sand represents less-essential priorities or tasks.

You need to fill your jar with rocks first, or else you will be stuck with a jar full of sand, and no room for anything else.

You will have to actively fight to reserve time for your high-priority items, because sand will come seeping in from all sides. Sand is not just junk. It can include worthy or enjoyable activities that you just don't have time for if you are going to accomplish your high-priority goals. Sand can be generated by your own initiative or by requests for assistance from other people. To find time to write this book, I have had to leave housework undone until my writing time was over, say no to some committees and school requests, turn off the television, unplug the telephone, leave e-mail unanswered, and decline many appealing social invitations.

Many clichés begin with the phrase "At the end of my life, I will look back and wish I had spent more time . . ." I am pretty sure that no one on his or her deathbed ever completed this thought with "I wish I had watched more television" or "I wished I had surfed the Internet more," yet on a daily basis we are confronted with many tempting time wasters. To save money, you need to pay yourself first. To save time, you need to schedule yourself first. Give your highest-priority activities a protected status on your calendar. Put appointments like your own health checkups on your calendar well ahead of time, and don't allow yourself to cancel your self-care schedule when inconvenient yet nonessential conflicts come up.

It takes discipline and focus to manage all of the things that you have to do, but by learning to do so, you will be greatly rewarded with a life that is full of fun, meaning, and growth for yourself and your family.

Phase Four: Baby Steps Toward Your Goals

As this process unfolds, you may develop some big goals that will take time to fulfill, as well as smaller changes that you can implement now. If you are staying at home but have an idea for a career you'd like to rejoin or start in the future, take time to research that field, and think about signing up for a reasonable schedule of additional training you may need or volunteer opportunities to keep your skills honed. If you are employed as well as fulfilling home obligations, you may focus on achieving balance in a hectic schedule and making sure there is still time reserved for yourself. I recommend thinking about this as a daily focus on eating well and getting enough sleep and exercise, and a more substantial break for yourself at least once a week to do an activity you enjoy on your own, with friends, or with your partner.

A good way to deepen your relationships with your female friends is to get together as a group to discuss your long-term goals. This is, of course, also an excellent discussion to have with your life partner, but sometimes I prefer to brainstorm with my girlfriends first to decide what I want to do, and then talk to my problem-solving husband about how to reach that concrete goal.

Come up with a list of initial steps you can reasonably take to head in the direction of your dreams, creating a timeline of short-, medium-, and long-term goals. If you start preparing now, when the day arrives that your children are ready for their own independent schedules away from home (whether that is day care or school), you will be ready to take larger strides toward your own goals.

✳ Mojo Activities

Many of these activities can be done by yourself but are more effective if you do them with a group of trusted friends:

- Take stock of your activities, obligations, and priorities. On a big piece of paper list all of the activities you regularly include in your schedule. Include specific housework and parenting tasks. Look over your calendar to make sure you capture all that you do, and don't forget to count the tasks you perform when you feel like you're doing nothing—the work you do that is so ever-present and automatic that it doesn't make it onto a to-do list. You may be amazed by how long your list is. Label each activity as fun, meaningful, or absolutely necessary, or none of the above.

- Can you cross off the items on your to-do list that you have identified as neither fun, nor meaningful, nor absolutely necessary, and gracefully bow out of those obligations? Remember that you are not doing anyone a favor by taking on jobs that you can't give your full attention. Have the courage to say no, or even, "I made a mistake by taking on this responsibility. Can I help you find someone else to take over this task?" Practice this by role-playing saying no with friends.
- What do you want more of in your life? On your list of priorities, add time for yourself, time for your own interests and goals, and time alone with your partner if it's not already on your list.
- Get together with your friends for a Moms' night out to give voice to each woman's goals, and brainstorm ways to begin to move toward them. Commit to supporting one another as you move forward. Your friends may have connections and ideas that can help propel you toward destinations that now seem unattainable. The very act of expressing your goals to a group of trusted friends may give you the extra motivation you need to get started.
- If there is an element of your "former life" that you really miss but cannot bring back in the same form, discuss the essence of what you enjoyed about that activity. Then brainstorm ideas for new outlets that could fulfill the same need.
- Hold a family meeting to discuss the changes that may need

to take place. Encourage your partner and kids to examine their priorities as well. Your family may be more than willing to give up being stressed and overscheduled in exchange for a more relaxed family life. If you encounter resistance to change, listen carefully to what your family has to say, but stand your ground and remind your family how important these requests are to you. This is a good time to point out that a happy, well-rested, balanced Mom will be a lot more fun to be around than a frazzled stress monster!

REFERENCES AND RESOURCES

Finding Your Own North Star by Martha Beck

Martha Beck's life coaching specializes in helping people use catalytic events to move toward more satisfying and meaningful lives. Her detailed program can be directly applied to the challenges of motherhood. She is a recovering stress addict who has become an unapologetic "anti–Martha Stewart" by choosing to put cooking on her do-*not*-do list.

It's Hard to Make a Difference When You Can't Find Your Keys by Marilyn Paul

Marilyn Paul's book takes a deep look at the causes of disorganization. If you are really interested in getting down to the hidden, maladaptive "benefits" that keep us disorganized, and to change your attitude and behaviors at their core, this book can be a real eye-opener. This beautifully written, thoughtful book will challenge you and has the potential to change your life in big ways if you let it. I especially like the chapter titled "Your Home Could Be Your

Castle" for its discussion on fairly delegating household responsibilities among all family members.

More Than a Mom: Living a Full and Balanced Life When Your Child Has Special Needs by Amy Baskin and Heather Fawcett

Mothers of special-needs children face even more challenges than other Moms in juggling caregiving priorities and still managing to find time for themselves. *More Than a Mom* is the essential resource for families who have children with developmental disabilities, mental health or learning issues, or chronic medical conditions.

The One-Life Solution: Reclaim Your Personal Life While Achieving Greater Professional Success by Henry Cloud

Moms understand that we have only one life, even if we fill many roles on a daily basis. Dr. Henry Cloud helps us make the most of our days and lives. He talks about integrating our professional and personal lives, while also setting boundaries that define our time and priorities. Cloud shows that rather than boxing us in, thoughtful boundaries can ultimately create more freedom.

Let Your Life Speak: Listening for the Voice of Vocation by Parker Palmer

This slim, wise book about vocation traces Palmer's quest to find his true calling. Given that my focus is on motherhood, I was surprised by how closely Parker Palmer's writing and core beliefs resonated with my own. He is a man of my father's generation, yet his writing connected with my concept of mojo as one's core source of power related to life's meaning.

CHAPTER 4

Am I Just Being Selfish? Letting Go of Guilt, Worry, and Anxiety

Be kinder to yourself than you think you should be.
—ZEN TEACHER CHERI HUBER

As you embark on your quest to reshape your life as a mother, guilt, worry, and anxiety may begin to creep in. Self-sacrifice is tightly woven into the fabric of our cultural definition of motherhood. "Mother" inherently implies a relationship between two people—how would you illustrate a mother without including a child in the picture? Therefore, it is not surprising that any attempt by mothers to carve out time away from their children to pursue their separate interests and identities can feel threatening to our deepest cultural conceptions of motherhood. Motherhood is supposed to be the ultimate selfless job, so women are conditioned to feel that it is wrong for a mother to ask for something that is just for herself.

We can become enslaved to impossible ideals of being a perfect mother. I would challenge all of us to reject these images of self-denial and illusionary perfection. We may reflexively feel that a "self-centered" Mom is one of the most negative images we can imagine. What if we turn that idea on its head and ask what it would be like to be a Mom who has a "centered self"? Couldn't she still take good care of her family and herself? Wouldn't she be a healthier person, and more fun to be around?

Mothering can be backbreaking, mind-numbing, exhausting, sweaty, sticky, inequitable, endless, thankless work. Children can be rude, whiny, demanding, incessant, petulant, endlessly needy, unforgiving, and mean. (Bosses and partners can get that way too. So can mothers, for that matter!) It is inevitable that we will all experience bad days and ambivalent feelings. We, and our families, are only human, and feeling guilty about these normal emotions does not help anyone. At some point, life will become messy and complicated enough that all of our illusions of perfection are shattered. The challenge is to learn to love and embrace our imperfect lives as they are. Letting go of unwarranted guilt is an essential step in that process.

In my experience, guilt, and her evil stepsisters, worry and anxiety, are three of the most destructive and counterproductive human emotions. Their main effects are to make us feel unworthy and unhappy, without providing us with any useful information. Worry and guilt tend to come as a package deal—bundled together with self-sacrifice—in the invisible, cultural "Good Mother Emotions Starter Kit." Many mothers feel that "it's my job to worry about everyone." Constant worrying is ultimately corrosive, but worry can create a comforting illusion that we're accomplishing something, that somehow we can control life. In extreme cases, mothers cling to obsessive worry as a protective talisman and feel that if they stop worrying, then somehow disaster will slip in the door when they are not looking. The truth is that all this accomplishes is holding happiness at arm's length, so that we can never fully enjoy life. Becoming a parent puts us in a very vulnerable position. We will experience hurt and disappointment, even the possibility of loss and tragedy. Worrying about potential disasters will not protect us against any of these human experiences any more than a fear of flying will keep an airplane aloft.

An important lesson about the hazards of free-floating worry comes from the psychology of self-defense. In *The Gift of Fear*, safety expert Gavin de Becker makes a distinction between useless worry and the signal of true fear:

> *True fear is a gift that signals us in the presence of danger; thus it will be based on something you perceive in your environment or circumstance. Unwarranted fear or worry will always be based on something in your imagination or memory. Worry is the fear we manufacture; it is a choice. Conversely, true fear is involuntary; it will come and get our attention if necessary. But if a parent or child fears constantly, there is no signal left for when it's really needed. Thus, the parent who chooses to worry all the time or who invests unwarranted fears into children is actually making them less safe. Worry is not a precaution; it is the opposite because it delays and discourages constructive action. (pp. 44–45)*

Worry is a constant barrage of static noise that distracts us, while true fear is a clear bell ringing to warn us of real danger. If we turn down the static, we will improve our ability to hear and react to the bell when necessary.

🌟 Guilt—The Mother of All Emotions

The word "guilt" comes from the root word for "gold," referring to the penalty that is paid for a criminal offense. How often does the punishment of Mom guilt truly fit the crime? Consider the personal costs of feeling guilty for not measuring up to an unrealistic image of the perfect mother. How much time and energy does that waste? How much stress does it create? What is the effect on our parenting, and our identities, of doubting ourselves and worrying that we don't measure up?

Mothers can feel guilty for just about anything that they think might be lacking. The complementary types of guilt felt by stay-at-home Moms and employed Moms reveal the vicious cycle of guilt and projection that we create for ourselves. I think of this cycle as "The grass is always greener on the other side of the fence, and I resent anyone whose grass is greener than mine."

Stay-at-home Moms may feel guilty or unworthy for being "just a Mom," for leaving behind their careers and intellectual lives, for not making money, or for not enjoying the opportunity to stay at home. If your family can afford to live on one salary, it can be the path of least resistance and convenient for the family as a whole to have one parent—usually Mom—stay home to take care of all of the family management needs and the bulk of the child-rearing work. In practice, women may not enjoy their end of the deal. It can be a shock to see how traditional gender roles introduce radical divergence into the formerly parallel life paths of husbands and wives. Having your "equal partner" fly off to an important meeting, leaving you alone in charge of a busy household, fills some women with feelings of jealousy, anger, or dread. Many women are surprised to find that despite their original intentions, they just don't enjoy staying at home. They miss the reward and stimulation of participating in a professional career. It is too bad that many of us feel that we are faced with all-or-nothing career decisions, because if we had access to year-long paid leave and a variety of flexible employment options, it would be more feasible to raise an infant and then resume paid work. My own experience as a stay-at-home caregiver was a mix of loving being a Mom and disliking the endless work of managing a household. This is a hard feeling to own up to, because it can feel as if you are saying you don't care about your family, but this assumption creates just another unproductive pang of guilt. Even though I worked in a very service-oriented career as a high school teacher, if I had been asked to leave my chosen profession to become a nanny, cook, chauffeur, janitor, and nurse, I would not have been very happy—in fact, I would have hated it without feeling guilty! These caregiving responsibilities are meaningful because I love my child and husband, not because I love all of these tasks or am particularly suited to them. As soon as my daughter entered preschool, I reworked my life to make my writing career one of my major priorities, and I began to feel less frustrated and more like myself again.

Employed Moms may feel guilty for not spending enough time with their children, for stepping off the fast track at work, or for not having the energy and time to devote to creating a perfect home. Unfortunately, the equal but opposite feelings of guilt experienced by employed Moms and stay-at-home Moms do not cancel each other out. Instead, they can pile up to create a real barrier—separating women into different camps—as these feelings of inadequacy in ourselves quickly swing around into judgments of others.

I have thought a lot about whether the so-called Mommy Wars have real substance or exist merely as a figment of the media's imagination. The flames of conflict are definitely fanned by the media, but I have to say that I do believe that most of us have taken a sliver of the Mommy Wars into our own hearts. This creates more guilt and discord, which are truly counterproductive feelings, whether they are directed toward ourselves or other women. It's worth becoming aware of these feelings and challenging the validity of the thoughts behind them. When you feel yourself judging another parent, I encourage you to take a moment to ask yourself whether you are really bothered by what that person is doing, or if your judgment is really a reflection of something happening in your own life. If it is really about your own life, is there something you need to change? Or is there an unrealistic expectation you need to let go of? How much more could we all accomplish as parents if we worked cooperatively for greater support for all types of families? Even after decades of feminism, women continue to struggle with the maze of options and obligations spread before us. The worst-case scenario would be that all of us feel guilty about our own choices or desires, and deprive ourselves of either the freedom to try doing something differently, or the pleasure of enjoying the life we have.

A sign that the Mojo Mom concept has caught on will be that Moms are able to fully support other women who have made different life-work choices.

I believe that at the core, we all want the same thing. Zen scholars teach that language is only "the finger pointing at the moon, not the moon itself." That's how I feel about the Mommy Wars. It's time to look beyond our fingers pointing at one another to get to the heart of the matter.

What Moms Really Want

- To be appreciated and have all our work recognized as important

  Much of the work we do is still invisible and unacknowledged. Housework and child rearing are demanding work, yet our efforts are most noticeable when things aren't going well. Stereotypically, men build skyscrapers and women clean them. No one ever looked at the Empire State Building and said, "Yeah, it's tall, but what's really amazing is how clean the bathrooms are." Whether we are in the boardroom or playing board games with our kids, we want to have that work recognized.

• To use our talents

Every woman deserves to have an opportunity to continue to use and develop her whole range of her talents. I have written about this on a practical level, but I believe it is also important on a personal, spiritual level as well. Motherhood taps a lot of our skills, but let's face it, every hardworking Mom needs a creative outlet that allows her to express herself and to let off steam in a new setting. We can do this on our own, through volunteer opportunities, or through continuing our careers.

Along with this desire I sense a fear among Moms that we are in danger of losing our sense of identity and losing our power. This can be expressed as jealousy or judgment of women who have followed different life-work paths, or an inability to honestly express our needs to our partners. When stay-at-home Moms talk about how useless their husbands are around the house, but how they just have to put up with that, I worry that we have given away our power and need to find ways to reclaim it within our relationships.

• To be recognized and to feel part of a group

Mothers form the largest sisterhood on earth—arguably the most important group that holds this whole enterprise together. In the best circumstances, being a member of this club creates an inclusive and supportive environment. However, this can cross over into exclusivity that hurts other women. There is a fine line between creating an environment among women who share common experiences and splitting up into cliques that make "other kinds of Moms" feel less worthy.

I have walked a similar line myself, as men have asked me why I create talks and seminars that are just for women. I believe that for better or worse, a mother's experience truly is different from a father's and there is value in talking about these issues among women. Whenever an exclusive group is created, though, I would ask the founders to carefully examine why the group is set up that way, whether it is truly justified, and who is being left out. Reaching out has value. While I continue to host all-women events, I have created a separate Mojo Families talk to present to mothers and fathers.

- To know that we are doing a good job as Moms

Here's the real heart of the Mommy Wars. I don't believe that most women are really so worried that other kinds of Moms are doing a bad job and are hurting their kids by making different choices about working or staying at home. I think that each of us at our very core of our being wants to know that we are doing a good job ourselves—not just keeping things together and being somewhat appreciated for it, but doing things *right*. All throughout our academic studies and our professional careers, we knew how we were doing. We got an A on a report, a raise, kudos from our boss, awards, recognition.

As mothers, not only do we receive scant praise, but we are faced with a daunting task whose final results won't be known for at least twenty years. Many women have been raised to aim for perfection, and as mothers we take on a role that is impossible to do perfectly. Perfect motherhood is a puzzle as insolvable as the Zen paradox that asks the question, "What is the sound of one hand clapping?" Even more maddeningly for those of us used to being totally in charge of our lives, the ultimate outcome of our work is largely out of our direct control. Raising children is an act of faith and requires courage. The famous quote by Elizabeth Stone says it best: "Making the decision to have a child—it's momentous. It is to decide forever to have your heart go walking outside your body."

To end the Mommy Wars within ourselves requires a new kind of thinking, one that gets us away from the corporate-ladder mentality and into the present moment of our lives. Extending compassion to ourselves and other women is the first step. Every Mom deserves a break, with the recognition that with few exceptions, we're all doing the best we can with what life has given us.

Who Can Give Us What We Want?

There is a lot that others can do to give us what we want. Society can decide to make women's work count on a number of levels, from categorizing homemakers as working instead of unemployed, to adopting caregiver-friendly public policies. Our families can honor what we do by both appreciating our work and pitching in to create a fully involved family work effort at home. But in the end, I believe that only we mothers can end the Mommy Wars. I urge each Mom to treat herself with the kindness she'd extend to her best friend, and to offer support rather than criticism to other mothers whenever possible. We are truly all in this together—sisters, not adversaries.

Mom Guilt in an Age of Hyperparenting

A final contributing factor to Mom guilt is the cultural trend toward overinvolved hyperparenting. This can happen to anyone: Employed Moms may adopt this tendency to make up for lost time with their children, and stay-at-home Moms may become overinvolved to justify their time spent away from the paid workforce. The current parenting zeitgeist seems to continually sweep us in this direction. A savvy editor pointed out to me that the new term "full-time Mom" may sound more positive than the older label "housewife," but at least "housewife" had a more narrowly defined scope than our current 24/7 image of what it means to be a "full-time Mom." When my generation was growing up in the seventies, our Moms were able to turn us loose knowing that we'd find someone to play with until it was time to come in for dinner. Part of this was due to the times, when it was more acceptable to have a band of kids running around the neighborhood with little adult supervision. Now our culture has evolved toward a child-centered structure that demands time together to enrich our children's learning as well as to protect their safety. Mommy and Me classes can be great, but it is also important to teach our kids to entertain themselves on their own, and to learn to play with other children without constant adult input. Add in the commercial pressure of experts and products designed to help us produce a smarter, healthier, happier child, and it's no wonder we all feel a little crazy sometimes. Even as Baby Einstein videos have been debunked as unnecessary and ineffective, there is no shortage of new products claiming to be the latest and greatest scientific breakthrough.

Take the BabyPlus "prenatal education system." Hey, I guess a regular baby isn't good enough anymore. You need to produce a baby PLUS. This has to win a prize for the most intrusive baby gadget. A pregnant woman in supposed to strap this little pulsating gizmo to her belly for two hours per day to give her *fetus* a jump-start on academic achievement. Promotional material proclaims that the BabyPlus device "introduces patterns of sound to the unborn child in the only language he or she understands—the maternal heartbeat." As if the developing fetus wasn't already hearing a heartbeat, the BabyPlus adds some sort of rhythmically enriched tonal patterns. The promised benefits include better sleep, better nursing, more self-soothing . . . right up to improved school readiness.

The BabyPlus ad in *Fit Pregnancy* magazine takes the promise of prenatal certainties even further. The pregnant model says, "I know it's a boy. I know his name is Ryan. I know he will be calmer, happier, and brighter because of BabyPlus."

Might as well decorate Ryan's nursery as a Tar Heels fan and send in his application to UNC. The truth is that you can't really know a child's personality or abilities ahead of time, no matter what you do.

So many high-tech products promise to take the uncertainty out of pregnancy or parenting. That idea may make us feel better now, but the empty promises ultimately set us up for more disappointment and guilt later. The marketing messages play on the worries generated by the inherent uncertainties of childbirth. This blurb for BabyPlus appeared as a What's Hot for Tots Web site "Featured Review" that blurs the fine line between editorial and advertorial content:

> *From the moment you find out you are going to be a mom the worries and concerns in your head go wild. You wonder and pray . . . will they be healthy, will they be a good baby, will they nurse, and will they sleep . . . and so on. Then you wonder about their milestones and childhood development; it is a natural thought process every mom and dad goes through. I am expecting my third and I try to do everything that is important for the health of my unborn baby. As I take my daily prenatal vitamins I think of our child's daily prenatal environment.*
>
> *That is why I am so happy to have the BabyPlus education system. When I came across this product I knew it was important for my unborn child's development.*

It angers me to see commercial companies taking advantage of the normal feelings of vulnerability that expectant parents have. If a pregnant woman wasn't already feeling anxious, that "review" sure suggests a lot to worry about. The truth is that BabyPlus can't promise that your baby won't be colicky, or that your child won't grow up to have dyslexia, ADD, or adjustment issues at school. BabyPlus can't guarantee a stable marriage, secure finances, siblings who get along, or healthy grandparents. When your ten-year-old shoplifts, is Baby-Plus going to be there to help you explain why that's wrong? At that point it's not going to help to say, "Ryan, BabyPlus babies don't steal." Parenting is an art as much as a science, and no gadget can trump the on-the-job training we will receive.

Anxious, overinvolved parenting is exhausting, and a long-term danger is that we as parents feel responsible for controlling exactly how our children turn out, providing us a nonstop ticket to the land of Mom guilt and worry. In her book *Perfect Madness*, Judith Warner describes our current state of anxiety as "that caught-by-the-throat feeling that so many mothers have today of *always* doing something wrong . . . The feeling has many faces, but it doesn't really have a name. It's not depression. It's not oppression. It's a mix of things, a kind of too-muchness. It's existential discomfort. A mess."

What's the alternative to this mess? Becoming a Mojo Mom calls for a bit of cultural rebellion. We need to take a step back and look at our culture, and make conscious decisions about what is right for our own families. We can give ourselves permission to stop competing with our neighbors—after all, who really knows if they are happy, secure, or financially solvent behind their public images? And there is solace in accepting the reality that there is no such thing as a perfect mother. Imperfection is part of the deal, and feeling overwhelmed or frustrated at times just means we are normal. It is a real challenge to accept that so much of motherhood is out of our direct control, but many mothers have reported gaining peace and strength by learning that *what we can't change, we can get through.*

Family life is often about finding a way to make peace with chaos, rather than making the chaos go away. Some of the most enjoyable times with our kids can come when we learn to go with the flow. From time to time it pays to say yes to crazy fun—even if it means that everyone jumps into the pool fully clothed. And if we are ever going to find some precious time to ourselves, we are going to have to accept that household chaos is a never-ending cycle. Housework is rarely, if ever, truly complete, and sometimes you need to let that work wait in order to get a moment to yourself. A Mojo Mom knows that sometimes a messy house means that you are busy doing something more important.

It may be helpful to consider the fact that your parenting is only one of many important influences in your child's life. In 1998, author Judith Harris turned conventional wisdom on its head by theorizing that parents are *not* the primary source of environmental influence on their children. Instead, her review of decades of psychological studies led her to conclude that peer group influence is a much more powerful factor than parental influence. Big differences in family environment—income, educational opportunity, absence of abuse—matter, but Harris argues that specific parenting styles just don't have that much influence on how children turn out as adults. Instead, she concludes that a child's peer group is a much greater influence than parental action. Harris's book, *The Nurture Assumption*, is worth reviewing to see if you find her case to be persuasive. Parents cannot claim total credit for their children's successes or guilt for all of their failures. My consideration of Harris's work is not meant to encourage sloppy parenting, but to bring balance to the conversation. I encourage good parents to accept the fact that neither they nor their children are perfect, and to celebrate the fact that they really are doing a great job.

Life coach and mother of three Melinda Abrams shares her wise perspective on why it is necessary and important to expand our children's circle of care beyond one set of exhausted parents:

Here's a huge mind shift that I had. With my background in education and coaching I have very strong beliefs about what I want my children to learn. It is essential to me that they learn critical and creative thinking skills, that they learn how to be kind and thoughtful, and that they are treated, and treat others, with respect. I want them to always know that they have a choice and that they have the ability to make good choices. I want them to learn the language to do all of these things. Coupled with all of that is the desire that they learn and grow in a peaceful environment.

The shift I had occurred after the birth of my second child. I can want all of that, and I can cultivate all of that, and I can't do it all by myself. I can hire babysitters who have skills and energy similar to Jeff's and mine. I want my children to know that they can thrive both with ourselves and with others. I want them to know that other people will support them with complete devotion, just like their Mom and Dad. It's my role to make sure I find those people to be in their lives and allow them to cultivate those relationships when I'm not there. The kids need to learn that. I need the time to cultivate myself away from them. It's a win-win.

Why Motherhood Is Not "The Most Important Job in the World"

Motherhood is often called "the most important job in the world," but I disagree. It's not because motherhood is not important, and I fully acknowledge that mothering is genuine, valuable work. However, on a personal identity level, Judith Stadtman Tucker, founder of the Mothers Movement Online, introduced me to the revelatory idea that *motherhood is not a job; it is a relationship.*

Buuuuuut . . . you protest, I work so hard at motherhood. I have so many professional skills and talents, and I am applying them to motherhood, so why shouldn't I view motherhood as my new career?

I know that feeling. I was there myself during my years as a stay-at-home Mom. You'll find support for this idea from authors like Darla Shine. In addition to writing the book *Happy Housewives*, Shine was affiliated with the short-lived magazine *Total 180!* "from briefcase to diaper bag," which was founded on the premise of Mom finding fulfillment in her new role as a "Chief Household Officer."

The problem is that if you look at motherhood as a professional outlet, you will start to expect motherhood to deliver the same rewards that a career does: measurable achievement, results, and advancement, and a sense of identity as you live your life through that role. Motherhood can deliver some of these feelings on a short-term basis, but it will ultimately disappoint you if that's what you are expecting from it. You can start living through your children as your "product," as their achievements become the justification and proof of your hard work. A headlong collision with disappointment and resentment is nearly inevitable, if you are ultimately expecting something that motherhood shouldn't have to deliver. Your professional mojo needs another outlet.

Look at it this way—what if we substitute "wife" for "mother" in this scenario. Imagine saying "My husband is my top priority. I quit my job so that I can give him one hundred percent of my attention. I feel guilty anytime I am not there for him. Hey, I have lots of professional skills, and now I put them to work at home. Being Michael's wife is the most important job I'll ever have."

That sounds blessedly unimaginable to most of us. The bottom line is, it is not fair to our spouses or children to expect them to fulfill us and form the basis of our identity. No one can deliver that, and it is wrong to ask. We need to be able to be with our children, and away from them, managing that delicate balance of connection without overpowering intrusion. Too close and we stifle each other. Too far away and we lose our connection.

I support stay-at-home Moms. I was one myself. But staying at home is not a one-way street into a cul-de-sac that must define the rest of your life. Even if you are absolutely in love with being at home with little ones, please don't burn your bridges to the rest of the world. Maintain your professional skills and contacts. You never know when you will need, or want, to go back to work. In the meantime, I urge you to commit to enjoying and cherishing the relationships with your family, but resist the temptation to lose yourself in them.

What Are the Antidotes to a Guilt-Ridden, Anxious Existence?

Melinda developed her perspective through experience as a coach and parent. For new Moms, a guilt-ridden, anxious existence is, unfortunately, a pretty natural outcome of the socialization and conditioning that most of us have received throughout our lives. If we are going to have a different experience, we need to make thoughtful choices that are different from the unconscious reactions and beliefs that have controlled us up to this point. The fact that becoming a mother brings us face-to-face with some of the most powerful socialization we will ever encounter is part of what makes it both a daunting challenge and an incredible opportunity for growth. Acceptance, gratitude, confidence, and compassion are tools that can help us move toward the goal of conscious living.

The transition to motherhood can be a difficult reality to accept, especially when it does not match up to our expectations. This was definitely my biggest struggle as a new Mom. I still don't know exactly where my expectations came from, but in retrospect, I see that they were incredibly unrealistic fantasies. (Douglas and Michaels's *The Mommy Myth* provides an extensive analysis of the societal pressures, media images, and public policies that feed these unrealistic ideals. These myths are not just the product of our own individual imaginations.) I went into motherhood with a full heart but little child-care experience, and without many friends who already had children. In my "life before baby," I worked as a scientist and teacher in a career that was incredibly social, rewarding, and demanding. My husband worked even longer hours than I did. He traveled extensively, and with the differences in our salary and work experience, there was no doubt that of the two of us, he would continue to be the primary breadwinner. I finished out my final year of teaching, planning to take a semester off, and expected to enjoy my time nesting at home with my newborn. I imagined that my baby would sleep well, for long periods of time, giving me a chance to have alone time to relax, work on my own projects, or do household chores at my leisure. I had a vague idea that I'd go back to teaching in some form, within a year.

After a healthy pregnancy and delivery, reality set in. During the early months, the physical demands of around-the-clock parenting of a newborn left me feeling foggy, sleepy, stupid, uninteresting, and not myself. I couldn't imagine stepping back into the demands of my full-time teaching job while in that state. Hours spent alone with a tiny baby felt unproductive and often lonely. Looking back at that time, I really can't tell you what we did all day, aside from breastfeeding, going to playgroups, and keeping the household minimally functioning.

And you know what? It turns out that as imperfect as this time was, that was okay. I made it through those first two crazy years, which also included a complicated cross-country move for our family. I eventually adapted, regained my bearings, and moved on to a much more satisfying, balanced lifestyle. As my daughter grew into an interactive toddler, then preschooler, we expanded the variety of activities we could do together. Much of what was so hard, though, was letting go of my expectations and dealing with the overwhelming nature of mothering, which I did not see coming. I had to let go of my romantic image of parenting and come to grips with the fact that my life had changed—permanently. My priorities were guided by a new star. Fantasies of equal parenting just did not square with my particular reality as the Mom of a newborn. For this period of her life, I was by far the primary caregiver. Whatever I thought mothering *should* be, this was my reality in my role as a stay-at-home Mom. Even if it was a life I had not expected, it was the life I now had.

> *It's not a matter of expecting less or expecting more,*
> *expecting the best or expecting the worst. Expecting*
> *anything just gets in the way of the experience itself. And the*
> *experience itself is a stunner.*
> —KAREN MAEZEN MILLER, *Momma Zen*

What is most interesting to me is that as difficult as it was, my new reality had a lot going for it. There was plenty of joy, laughter, fun, and cuddling to keep me going. It was that gap between what I expected and what I experienced that I felt had betrayed me. The two ways to deal with this situation are to change your expectations or change your reality. For my whole life, I'd always taken the proactive approach of controlling reality whenever possible. When motherhood just wouldn't conform to my expectations, I was faced with the unfamiliar task of accepting a new reality. For many overachieving Americans, acceptance feels like failure, but paradoxically, I found freedom in acceptance. The energy I put into struggling against motherhood was wasted. I was able to mold my life into a more satisfying existence only after I came to terms with the reality of my choices. Please remember that I am not advocating my specific choices as the only right ones, but I am encouraging you to accept your life as it is right now *as a starting point*, and move forward from there.

If the concept of acceptance feels weak or defeatist, consider the perspective given by Zen teacher Cheri Huber: "The acceptance I'm talking about is not failure, defeat, resignation, giving up, or a last resort. Also, my use of the word acceptance does not necessarily imply agreement or condoning" (*When You're Falling, Dive*, p. 2). Rather, Huber argues that acceptance is a key to freedom from the suffering we create for ourselves. Accepting our world as it actually is allows us to move beyond the limitations of our preconceived notions and opens up previously unimagined possibilities. Acceptance is also a precondition for change and action. Like worry, nonacceptance gives the illusion that we are doing something without actually accomplishing anything. Cheri Huber takes the approach that instead of wasting our energy resisting what is, "first we accept, then we get to work" (*When You're Falling, Dive*, p. 143). Her teachings are simple, yet they can radically change the way you look at the world. Her revolutionary notion that "you've been taught that there is something wrong with you and that you are imperfect, but there isn't, and you're not" is the jumping-off point to debunk much of the conditioning we have received as children and as parents. I highly recommend her books, especially *There Is Nothing Wrong with You*, as a starting point, and *When You're Falling, Dive: Acceptance, Freedom and Possibility* as a follow-up.

I am clearly not a Zen master, but mothering has turned me into a student. My baby showed me what it is like to live only in the present moment. She had no long-term goals or priorities. If she was happy now, she was happy, without worrying about the future, what other people thought of her, or whether she was getting enough done. I marveled at the fact that her very existence, without having any tangible accomplishments, brought joy to so many people. By becoming a Mom, I felt truly unconditional love for another person for the first time in my life, and I realized that my own parents loved me even more than I had ever known.

The biggest danger of measuring ourselves by how short we fall from reaching an unattainable standard of perfection is that we risk missing the blessings unfolding right now, before our very eyes. In school we all knew students who were bitterly disappointed if they received a B+. Some of us *were* those students, and in a school setting, that drive to settle for nothing less than an A may have helped us reach our academic goals. Evaluating our *lives* that way is no way to live. There is no final exam, only this day. If we can throw away our grade books, measuring sticks, and comparisons, we can appreciate the value of the gifts we have been given, most of us in utter abundance. We can accept ourselves and others, including our partners and children. We can see our family life as joy to be shared rather than just work to be divided and conquered. If there are changes that need to be made, we can make them rather than suffering in silence, chasing after elusive happiness that remains just beyond our grasp.

☀ Mojo Activities

I suggest the following exercise for Moms who are still having trouble making their own needs a priority:

Step 1: Think about the girl or woman in your life whom you are closest to who is not yet a mother. Imagine into the future that she is a grown, intelligent, accomplished woman, and that she is about to have her first child. Write her a letter full of your wisest advice, describing the kind of life you wish for her as a Mom. Read the letter out loud. (Do this before reading about the second step described on the next page.)

_____

_____

_____

_____

_____

_____

_____

_____

_____

_____

_____

_____

_____

_____

_____

_____

_____

_____

_____

_____

_____

_____

_____

_____

_____

_____

_____

Step 2: Now change the name at the top of the letter so that it is addressed to *you*. What have you wished for another cherished new Mom that you have not allowed yourself to ask for? Can you see that you need and deserve these good things as much as she would?

Take time to count your blessings and see the incredible value in your life rather than just deficiencies. How does the world look if you take a glass-is-half-full perspective?

_____

_____

_____

_____

_____

_____

_____

_____

_____

_____

_____

_____

_____

_____

_____

_____

_____

_____

_____

_____

☙ REFERENCES AND RESOURCES

When You're Falling, Dive; There Is Nothing Wrong with You; and *Time-Out for Parents* (with Melinda Guyol) by Cheri Huber

I love Cheri Huber's writing and recommend her work to every Mom. It doesn't really matter which book you read first, but I would start with *There Is Nothing Wrong with You. Time-Out for Parents* is a deceptively simple book that gets to the heart of two of the biggest ongoing challenges of parenting: being truly present with our children, and allowing them to experience all of their feelings, as well as allowing ourselves to feel our own emotions. As time passes, I appreciate the wisdom of Cheri Huber's message even more.

Momma Zen: Walking the Crooked Path of Motherhood by Karen Maezen Miller
Buddhism for Mothers and *Buddhism for Mothers of Young Children* by Sarah Napthali

These gems address the always-surprising spiritual path of motherhood. Karen Maezen Miller continues to share her writing through her Cheerio Road blog.

Mommy Guilt: Learn to Worry Less, Focus on What Matters Most, and Raise Happier Kids by Julie Bort, Aviva Pflock, and Devra Renner

If you are mired in mommy guilt, this thoughtful guide can help you find your way out. The book weaves in experiences of real Moms who responded to the authors' survey on mothering issues at a range of age levels and situations.

12 Simple Secrets Real Moms Know: Getting Back to Basics and Raising Happy Kids by Michele Borba, Ed.D.

There are so many good parenting books to choose from, but I especially appreciate Michele Borba's approach. She takes the latest research and distills it to its essence. She knows that we Moms can really make our role harder and more stressful than it has to be. Her advice helps you focus on what really matters most, then allow yourself to let the rest go.

Momfidence: An Oreo Never Killed Anybody and Other Secrets of Happier Parenting by Paula Spencer

Part parenting guide, part memoir, *Momfidence* can help lead you from insecurity to confidence, and help you laugh along the way.

Brain, Child: The Magazine for Thinking Mothers

Brain, Child takes a thoughtful, critical look at all aspects of motherhood and parenting, providing a very welcome alternative to the mythical view of motherhood provided by commercial, glossy, ad-filled magazines.

Protecting the Gift: Keeping Children and Teenagers Safe by Gavin de Becker

You can reduce your free-floating anxiety by learning solid information that will actually help keep your children safe and prevent abuse. Parents need this information from birth, so that they become their children's safety advocates and teachers. Gavin de Becker has written some of the best books on this topic, including *Protecting the Gift,* which is written specifically for parents.

Kidpower

Teaching our children real-world safety skills is one of the best antidotes to anxious, overinvolved "helicopter parenting." We can let our kids fly free once we are confident that they have the ability to navigate the world on their own. Kidpower-Teenpower-Fullpower International offers positive, success-based personal safety training for parents, caregivers, kids, and teens. I am proud to be a member of the Kidpower community as the Center Director for Kidpower North Carolina. To learn more about Kidpower training near you, visit www. Kidpower.org.

CHAPTER 5

Centering, Silence, and Reclaiming Your Mind Space

*The most precious gift we can offer others is
our presence. When mindfulness embraces those we love,
they will bloom like flowers.*

—THICH NHAT HANH

Free time is one of the rarest and most precious commodities for
a new Mom. Sure, Moms experience some quiet time at home
when the baby is asleep, but this alone time can be interrupted at any
second, and is often taken over by household duties, so it is not really
free. In the early months, many Moms will be concerned primarily
with the basic needs of physical recovery, sleeping, and eating. As we
become ready to leave the cocoon, it is important to set up regularly
scheduled time that is truly our own; time when we are free to lose
ourselves in our own thoughts, without having any responsibility to
anyone else. Lunch with a friend, or an hour alone at a coffee shop or
bookstore—things we all took for granted before becoming Moms—
can feel like an exotic getaway.

I consider slacking off to be a truly radical act for a mother, and a necessary one! (I highly recommend Ariel Gore's essay on this idea, "It Takes a Heap of Loafing to Raise a Kid," from her book *The Mother Trip*.) It is so easy to get caught up in a whirlwind, feeling that we always need to be doing something. This leads to endless running around and chronic stress. It can feel incredibly liberating to break this destructive cycle and settle back into our true centers, physically and spiritually. As with so many other things, you will have to make a conscious choice to make centering a priority, and to ask for the help you need to make this time available.

The spiritual, physical, and mental aspects of centering are all interconnected. Many families rediscover spirituality and religion after having children. I used to think this was just to pass on values to the children, but now I also realize how important spirituality is for my own well-being and development. A weekly hour spent in worship may be the only time some mothers have to enjoy attentive silence, contemplation, and recentering. Alternatively, mindfulness techniques or physical activities can help calm a racing mind and pull us back into our selves. It is helpful to develop a variety of centering techniques for yourself, especially as you encounter the specific challenges of different stages of mothering. As a new mother, you are, of necessity, close to your baby all day, so physical privacy and a chance to stretch out and exercise may be your biggest challenge. As children become verbal toddlers, then hyperverbal preschoolers, mental privacy becomes a major challenge.

My experience as the Mom of a preschooler, hearing "Mommy, Mommy, Mommy" all day, followed by various requests, demands, and questions (no matter how charming), has led me to formulate a concept that I call "reclaiming your mind space." Later in this chapter we will discuss in detail Mom-specific ideas to help you create a mental environment that allows your inner life to flourish.

☀ Activities to Center Your Mind and Body

Centering is the experience of settling your entire being, allowing yourself to relax physically and mentally into a place of inner strength and support. The mind and body are entwined in this process. You can initiate centering by allowing your mind to come to rest and your body to relax, or by developing a strong physical core to support you.

Meditation is the classic method of quieting the mind and following your thoughts with active, nonjudgmental awareness. Meditation is a wonderful discipline that I highly recommend, though I admit that I have not developed a formal practice. In fact, my ideas for reclaiming your mind space stem from how hard it was to find time to join a meditation group or start a discipline. Instead, I have looked for ways to create a meditative or enjoyable mental environment throughout my everyday routine. Spiritual leader Thich Nhat Hanh teaches that even a red traffic light can be transformed from a stressful signal into a conscious reminder to recenter ourselves. Mothers, in particular, benefit from small centering rituals integrated into our daily lives, so that we are present in each moment instead of mindlessly rushing from one task to the next. The reaction from those around us can be interesting. I started the practice of taking a deliberate moment to recenter myself with a deep, relaxing breath each time I parked the car. The very first time I tried this, my preschool-aged daughter called out from the backseat, "Mommy, you aren't allowed to rest." I was amazed that she had picked up on this two-second break as being something different in my routine, and I was taken aback that she did not think I was allowed to do so. This was a clear message that I needed to stop rushing so much, for both of our sakes.

Five Good Minutes
to Start Your Day

Dr. David Servan-Schreiber is a psychiatrist, neuroscientist—and brain cancer survivor. His book *Anticancer: A New Way of Life* focuses on diet, exercise, and other beneficial lifestyle changes. I was struck by his comments in the question-and-answer section of a November 2008 *Ode* magazine article:

> Q: What's the most important thing a person can do to prevent or fight cancer?
>
> A: That's a very tough question. I think most important is to take a little bit of time every day—maybe just five minutes—with yourself to listen to the life force in yourself, pay attention to it, nurture it and express your gratitude to it.
>
> Q: Taking five minutes a day doesn't sound difficult.
>
> A: Yes, it is. Taking your life seriously is difficult because we're not trained to express love for ourselves. But if you can't take just five minutes for yourself, I doubt you will be capable of changing your diet or changing your exercise pattern because you're not going to feel you're worth it. Connecting to the life force inside you will help you face the challenges and treat yourself better. Expressing this radical act of love is the step that leads to all other steps.

My initial introduction to the art of centering came through practicing aikido, a uniquely peaceful martial art that is based on the principle of nonresistance. O'Sensei, the founder of aikido, wanted to create a modern system that developed the alignment of body, mind, and spirit for every student. O'Sensei understood that continued fighting—with others, with ourselves, and with the environment—will ruin the earth: "What we need now are techniques of harmony, not those of contention. The Art of Peace is required, not the Art of War" (Ueshiba, *The Art of Peace*, pp. 8–9).

Instead of resisting the power of an attack head-on, aikido is based on redirecting your attacking partner's energy and blending it with your own energy and movements. While practicing, you are constantly reminded to keep yourself grounded and centered. Your feet maintain a connection with the ground, while energy reaches up throughout your body, extending through the top of your head, and out your fingertips. When you move, you move from your center, or *hara*, which is your place of stability and strength. Your *hara* is physically located in the abdominal area below your belly button—you know, the part of your belly that never seems to go back to the way it was before you had a baby. By connecting with your *hara*, you can learn to love that part of your body again, whether or not you'd ever wear a cutoff top and low-rise jeans. Your *hara* is your place of physical balance, stability, and power. With a woman's build, we have lower centers of gravity based around our hips. These are the parts of our bodies that are powerful and grounded. Sinking into your *hara* and having your moves originate from a solid base, instead of flailing about from your shoulders, or teetering on tiptoes, is a good way to feel centered. Learning fundamental aikido-based centering moves and visualizations, even if you don't adopt a long-term practice, can be valuable training. The inherent psychology of aikido—blending and redirecting energy instead of butting heads—can also teach us to develop a peaceful yet strong leadership style that helps us interact effectively with our children.

Parents can also benefit from learning the aikido concept of *mai*, which means maintaining the correct distance between yourself and your practice partner. You cannot practice aikido correctly if you are stepping on each other's toes, but you also can't work together if you stand out of arm's reach. The same can be said of parenting. Kahlil Gibran's classic poem "On Children" reminds us that

> *Your children are not your children.*
> *They are sons and daughters of Life's longing for itself.*
> *They come through you, but not from you,*
> *And though they are with you yet they belong not to you.*
>
> (THE PROPHET, P. 17)

Our children need to remain in the sphere of our guidance, but they cannot mature if they are not given opportunities to explore on their own and develop into the people they are meant to become. This creates one of the biggest ongoing challenges of parenthood. The delicate balance between connectedness and autonomy evolves over time, as children develop the skills that demonstrate that they are ready for more independence.

Validation of the importance of a strong physical core came when I learned Pilates, a series of strengthening exercises that are matched with controlled breathing patterns. In the Pilates system, the lower belly is considered to be the powerhouse, the place where all of your breathing originates. Pilates works to strengthen that core powerhouse, providing postural support for your entire body, and creating the nice side effect of flattening your belly. Pilates movements work very deeply, affecting breathing, ease of movement, and postural strength and alignment. All of these areas are easy to neglect as mothers. The physical demands of carrying babies and toddlers over months and years can really take their toll on your body. Pilates can help restore your flexibility, strength, and posture.

Yoga is an ancient and highly regarded method of stretching and strengthening your body while creating a mind-body connection. Yoga also focuses on the breath as a source of life, power, and strength. When we rush around in our daily lives, we may take only shallow breaths, and we may even catch ourselves holding our breath during periods of stress. Yoga training can teach us to take full, natural breaths, which fully support each cell in our bodies. The combination of stretching and breathing can release physical tension in our muscles while also calming our busy minds.

With any meditation, martial arts, or exercise program, the quality of your experience is highly linked to the quality of the teaching you receive. It is worth taking the time to investigate more than one teacher, and to check out each instructor's qualifications and experience. Yoga and Pilates, in particular, have become very trendy, so someone advertising a Pilates class may actually be a general fitness instructor who has had very little training in the Pilates method. It is also important to make sure that your instructor is willing to adapt the exercises to fit your personal level of experience and any physical limitations you might have. It is fine for an instructor to challenge you, but it is not okay to push you to hurt yourself, or for any teacher to try to take on the role of an all-powerful guru or bully who dictates your experience. This is your experience—precious time for yourself, when it is essential to feel supported in trusting your own boundaries, needs, and power.

Creating Physical Spaces for Silence and Reflection

All Moms need places to get away for a quiet or creative moment. Do you have a special place to retreat? Look first inside your home. Is there any space that is truly yours? A friend told me about the mansion that her wealthy father shares with his second wife and their two children. On the surface, her stepmother's touch is all over the beautifully decorated home. But if you look at what the rooms are actually used for, you realize that the kids have playrooms, Dad has multiple activity rooms dedicated to his hobbies, and his exercise equipment is in the master bedroom. Mom has only a small desk in an alcove that is set aside as hers. *All of us need space that is ours*—not just bill-paying space, but a place where we can enjoy sitting, relaxing, reading, and daydreaming. How can you create a space for yourself in your own home? It doesn't have to be a whole room. Your space could be a cozy chair in a revamped master bedroom that is reprioritized as a place for relaxation, romance, and retreat, instead of an exercise room or a place to watch television. It is up to you to decide what makes you feel safe, creative, and supported. Once you create your retreat, and visit it regularly, you will have a place where you can go to reconnect with yourself, whether you have five minutes or a free afternoon. Take care of your special place. Even if it is just a comfy chair in a corner, keep it cleared off and ready for you to arrive. If your special place is buried under laundry or papers, you won't even want to visit it.

While your special places at home are essential, there is only so much retreating you can do there, especially when your children are small. We all need a place to escape to, for an hour or two on our own or with a friend. I recommend exploring your town and finding a new place that you've never been before, or at least a place that you never

What About Your Home on Wheels?

Unless you are fortunate enough to have access to excellent public transit, you probably spend a great deal of time in your car, whether it is commuting to the office, running to the grocery store, or shuttling kids around to their activities. Anything you can do to make your car feel even a little bit special, a little bit *you*, can help create another opportunity for centering. You are going to be in the car anyway, so how can you make it your own? An opinionated bumper sticker, a personalized license plate, a flower vase in a cup holder, a dashboard toy—how can you make the car an environment that reflects your personality? If you listen to music in the car, make sure that you get a turn listening to your songs rather than getting stuck with an endless loop of Raffi or Kindermusik.

I have come to appreciate what a big part of my daily life my car is, and I recommitted myself to keeping it clean and uncluttered. It still gets into acute phases of disaster, where I feel like I am living inside a giant purse, but I have tried to become more mindful about keeping my car in good shape. Whether I'm alone or driving a carpool full of kids, I feel good knowing that my car can truly be "a room of my own"—my MojoMobile!

take your kids. I live in a small city, so I retreat to a coffeehouse a few miles away from my neighborhood where I am unlikely to run into someone I know. I can be alone to read, meet a girlfriend for grown-up conversation, or take my laptop computer and write. It's really important to me that it's not the same place where I take my daughter. When she and I go out to get coffee for me and hot chocolate for her, we visit a different coffeehouse just a few blocks away. The kid-friendly chain is "our" place, while my secret bohemian retreat up the road is "my" place.

Finding time alone with your spouse or partner when you can re-connect as yourselves, and not just as parents, is absolutely essential to the growth of your relationship. We will devote an entire chapter to these challenges when we get to Chapter 7: "Daddies as Mojo Partners."

✻ Reclaiming Your Mind Space

Creating these physical spaces merges into the process that I have named "reclaiming your mind space," which involves creating a selective mental environment that lets in what you wish to experience and filters out chaos. The need to reclaim your mind space arises from our overwhelming media and consumer culture as much as it does from being a mother. However, becoming a Mom made me acutely aware of this need, as I had to fight for any sense of mental privacy and serenity. My daughter turned up the volume in my life—which is just what kids do!—and the solution wasn't to quiet her down, but to think more carefully about the other inputs in my life that were creating mental clutter and a sense of feeling overwhelmed.

We are all bombarded by an insane number of messages, images, and ads every day. Much of what we are exposed to through the mainstream media is violent, sexual, or both. News is sensationalized and focused on what is novel or scandalous, rather than what is truly important. These days it can be hard to distinguish CNN from SoapNet as the news cycle gyrates through the scandals of the day.

In our information age we are unhealthily desensitized to what we see. Back in 1913, a riot broke out during the first ballet performance of Igor Stravinsky's *The Rite of Spring*. Audiences, accustomed to the demure conventions of classical ballet, were shocked by the violent dance steps depicting fertility rites. We've come a long way since then. A reconstructed performance of this ballet was performed on PBS in 1988, causing some channel changing, but from boredom rather than shock.

Today it is difficult to turn off the media bombardment. If you are not aware how graphic music content has become, watch a few music videos and read the lyrics to Eminem's "Kim," his disturbing fantasy of murdering his wife, or Missy Elliott's very sexually explicit "Work It." If you can get past Britney Spears, skanky clothing in the girls' 6x–12 department at major department stores, the gross-outs of *Fear Factor*, the casual sexuality of *The Real World* and *The Bachelor*, not to mention all the sex and violence at your local movie theater, you are still left with the CNN news crawl on TVs in your line of vision in many public places. It takes a concerted effort to unplug from this barrage of emotionally charged information. It is tempting to just zone out and convince ourselves that these inputs have no real effect on us. However, the truth is that our mental environment does shape our brains, those of adults as well as children, who have the additional challenge of processing this information without the life experience to understand it or put it in context.

In his book *The New Brain: How the Modern Age Is Rewiring Your Mind,* neuroscientist Richard Restak tells us that while we may intellectually think that explicit or violent images wash right over us, the more primitive parts of our brain that process fear and emotion react to these images as though they were actual threats, increasing our levels of stress and anxiety. Our entire nation was justifiably traumatized by the terrorist attacks of September 11, 2001, but our trauma was compounded by the endless replays of video clips of the World Trade

Center towers collapsing and the crash sites in Pennsylvania and the Pentagon. Studies have found a correlation between how much television coverage people watched after 9/11 and their likelihood of suffering from post-traumatic stress disorder.

Overexposure to the media onslaught can leave us traumatized and desensitized. I urge you to make a conscious decision for yourself and your family to monitor what you consume with your minds as carefully as you watch your family's nutrition. We need to act as our own filters to avoid bingeing on media sex and violence. I am not asking you to shut out the rest of the world, but rather to take in information carefully, and nontraumatically, in servings that you can really think about. My approach is about turning down the volume on the things you don't want to consume, and turning up the volume on things you find interesting, important, and enjoyable.

Here are my suggestions for reclaiming your mind space. I encourage you to try the ideas that seem feasible for you.

- Begin to notice your own modes of sensing and thinking, and create opportunities to use your mind in different ways. As a writer, I enjoy getting engrossed in my work, but I can get stuck spending too much time in the abstract "thinking" world inside my head. As a mother I try to live in the present when I am with my daughter. Living in the moment when she was a baby and toddler felt like a Zen exercise. It was wonderful, but I also missed having my private thinking time. Do you have opportunities to get lost in your thoughts, as well as living in the sensory here and now? Do you have a chance to stretch your mind in different ways, spiritually, creatively, and mindfully?
- Turn off background TV. Many advocates would say turn it off altogether, but I can't go that far myself. I happen to love TV and movies, but I try to watch TV only when I have a specific show I am interested in. I definitely recommend that you turn

off the TV during family meals or other activities, and that you discourage mindless channel surfing. TiVo/digital video recorder (DVR) technology can help you watch selectively. You can record shows, and then watch them on your time, or you can just start watching an hour-long show twenty minutes after it has started, and catch up with real time as you fast-forward through the ads. The one potential downside of a DVR is that it means there is almost always something available to watch, so it's tempting to allow kids to watch more TV, or for parents to watch TV all evening after the kids are in bed. But there is no doubt that a DVR can be a great tool to enable selective TV watching. TiVo is the best-known brand DVR, but there are others available, including services offered directly from your existing cable company. I knew that this technology had reached the tipping point of acceptance by the next generation, at least, when my daughter asked me why she couldn't pause the shows on Grannie's set, and I had to explain to her what "live TV" was.

- Think carefully about how you want to consume news. Television, radio, and newspapers and magazines provide very different ways to take in the news. TV news is sensational and filled with commercials. It is important to realize that while watching TV news, it is difficult to avoid news stories that you don't want to hear (unless you play back a recorded show). I prefer reading the newspaper, because I can find out what is going on by reading the headlines while skipping over the gory details of violent crimes. The newspaper also provides an outlet for more thoughtful opinion pieces and in-depth coverage than the medium of TV permits. Consuming print media rather than television news also protects you from being exposed to endless video loops of bad news you have already heard about.

- As for news radio, you can find a wide range of quality and opinion there. I am a big fan of National Public Radio (NPR). The lab manager played public radio in our workspace all day long during my six years of graduate school, so I basically had to get on board or go nuts. NPR and other public radio contributors provide thoughtful news coverage, brilliant interview and documentary shows such as *This American Life* and *Fresh Air*, and the comic relief of *Car Talk*, in a low-commercial environment.

- Take advantage of new ways to access the content you really like. The upside to the information age is that it is possible to customize our media content to access the things we do want to hear about. iPods have transformed listening the way TiVo has transformed television, allowing us to bring our music, news, audiobooks, and video with us wherever we go. I enjoy most of my public radio listening through podcasts I download to my iPod and listen to while cleaning the house or walking the dog. This is the one kind of multitasking I really enjoy. My love for public radio led me to create my own show, *The Mojo Mom Podcast*, which features guest interviews with leading motherhood authors and newsmakers. You can access our archived episodes free through MojoMom.com or iTunes.

- As far as music goes, in addition to creating my own playlists, I found that it is very useful to make Mom/kid mixes that contain songs we both enjoy listening to on the go. This allows me to easily switch back and forth between my alone-time content and our together-time music without overloading my car with CDs. When my daughter was a toddler, I made the mistake of playing kids' music in the car too often. Long after the novelty of kids' music had worn off for me, my daughter was so used to her songs that she would throw a fit if I tried to play songs that I liked (what's familiar is preferred). As a compromise, I now make playlists that alternate between her music and my music. I edit out the particular songs that I can't stand from her albums, and I put in songs from my music collection that I know she thinks are okay—like Jack Black in *School of Rock*, for the preschool set.

Finding time and space for silence, centering, and reclaiming your mind space can be a challenge, but if you make it a priority, you can do it. When you give your mind time and freedom to roam, you may find new sparks of emotion and creativity igniting. We'll explore ways to play with that creative energy in the next chapter.

REFERENCES AND RESOURCES

Dojo Wisdom for Mothers: 100 Simple Ways to Become a Calmer, Happier, More Loving Parent by Jennifer Lawler

Black belt Jennifer Lawler applies the lessons of her martial arts training to the challenges of motherhood.

Mommy Mantras: Affirmations and Insights to Keep You from Losing Your Mind by Bethany Casarjian and Diane Dillon

Even if you're not the mantra type, mommy mantras are useful phrases you can say in your head, or out loud if you need to, during those trying moments of mothering. They act to empower you, revive you, and remind you that there is always another way to see your situation.

Meditation Secrets for Women: Discovering Your Passion, Pleasure, and Inner Peace by Camille Maurine and Lorin Roche

Maurine and Roche explore the reasons why women do not always fit into the male model of meditation practice. They have developed techniques that take women's specific needs and strengths into account.

The Soft Addiction Solution: Break Free of the Seemingly Harmless Habits That Keep You From the Life You Want by Judith Wright

Soft addictions are socially sanctioned habits like shopping, watching television, and surfing the Internet. If you are having a hard time focusing on your vision for the future and wish you could carve more purpose and meaning out of your crowded days, Judith Wright's plan can help you cut out the wasteful habits that distract us from our real feelings and genuine experiences.

The Woman's Retreat Book by Jennifer Louden

Jennifer Louden's book is a great resource for retreats of all lengths, ceremonies, and activities to do alone or with a group.

The Prophet by Kahlil Gibran

This slim volume is Lebanese philosopher Gibran's masterpiece of poetic wisdom. It has been said of Gibran that "his power came from some great reservoir of spiritual life or else it could not have been so universal and so potent, but the majesty and beauty of the language with which he clothed it were all his own."

At the Root of This Longing: Reconciling a Spiritual Hunger and a Feminist Thirst by Carol Lee Flinders

Flinders has spent much of her career studying female Christian mystics, and for a time she lived in a meditation community based on Eastern philosophy. Flinders explores the apparent conflicts between feminism and spirituality. Her inspiring conclusion is that a life of meaning, self-knowledge, and freedom depends on the realization that feminism and spirituality are more than just compatible—they are mutually necessary. I highly recommend this profound and challenging, but highly readable book. It would make an excellent book club selection for a group interested in exploring these issues.

 Express Yourself

Art is the only way to run away without leaving home.

—TWYLA THARP

To reclaim your mojo, it is essential to allow yourself to experience your true feelings, and find an outlet to express them. It can be scary to really feel your emotions without judging them or pushing them away. Because motherhood is such an intense role, there inevitably will be times that you don't like your children, your partner, or yourself very much. Creative expression is a tool we can use to chip away at the dangerous taboo against expression that threatens to turn Moms into emotionally repressed zombies. This is important work on many levels. A woman's unexpressed needs and feelings can crystallize into irreversible resentment over time, which is unhealthy for the whole family.

Growing up socialized as girls and women, we may have learned that it is not okay to express negative feelings, and we may not know *how* to. Strategies of pushing feelings aside that worked before will most likely not work when faced with the intense, ongoing challenges of parenting. If you've never really learned how to deal with anger, pain, and frustration, now is the time to develop these skills. As a parent, you will need to deal with your children's misbehavior (accidental and intentional), having your buttons pushed, having your plans changed or ruined, putting your own needs aside, the exhaustion of sleep deprivation, and the physical pain of inevitable accidental bumps and bruises you will receive from your child. Many of us were never challenged like this before we became parents. As with so much in parenting, this crisis can be seen as a danger or an opportunity. We are faced with the danger of running away from our feelings to escape into numbed lives, or the scary but wonderful opportunity of really waking up, perhaps for the first time ever.

We can change the way we deal with emotions even if we didn't learn how to do so as children. My parents' families never met an emotion they couldn't stuff back down. On both sides, my family is made up of many wonderful people whom I love dearly. As a system, though, my extended family suffers from a severe case of stoic repression, thickly shellacked with a veneer of projected perfection. In earlier generations, there was a great deal of emphasis placed on creating a positive outward image, regardless of the actual conflicts going on within. A "buck up, Buttercup" type of reaction to an expressed emotion or problem can work occasionally, but as a family's primary coping mechanism, it serves the function of clamping on each person's mask of inauthenticity.

A large part of growing up is learning to transcend the limitations of our families of origin. Now that we are parents, we have the opportunity and responsibility to acquire the expressive skills we want to give to our children. Change is possible within extended families, as well. Being a Mom, and getting my mojo back, has given me the courage to see the world as it really is, rather than always clumsily trying to force life to conform to my expectations. This has led me to be more open with family members of all ages. As I have become willing to enter more honest relationships, my family has been more willing to offer them. I urge you to take a fresh look at your own parents through adult eyes. Consider forgiving them for their failings and thanking them for their accomplishments. What old grievances are you holding on to? Can you find a way to express them, if necessary, to find closure, or to choose to let them go? No matter how justified we are in our grievances, a lifetime accumulation of hurt is like a fist full of tacks. The tighter we squeeze, the more we hurt ourselves. If we relax our clenched fist, we alleviate our pain. When we release the tacks, we can regain full, free use of our hands.

A Mom who loses herself, and has no safe emotional outlets, has a long way to fall. Without support or coping mechanisms, many mothers turn to literally anesthetizing themselves with alcohol or other drugs. An estimated 5 million American women have crossed the line into problem drinking. A thirty-year-old alcoholic Mom, whose two children were seven and four years old, described her drinking this way on *The Oprah Winfrey Show*:

> *There gets to be a point where I can't wear this mask any more, of pleasantness, and I want so badly to be pleasant to those in my life, and giving. I get to a point where I can feel that I am just getting so uncomfortable with the emotions inside—which I logically know are very human emotions—stress, frustration, exhaustion. And I logically know the right things I should do, but what I really want, to calm it quickly, is alcohol. And I can feel the tingle. I would say after two drinks, I can literally feel going from skin crawling to just this warm tingle coming through me.*
> (The Oprah Winfrey Show, April 19, 2004)

Without outlets for expression, coping mechanisms, and support, the escape into predictable, comforting numbness can seem like the only option, even if we realize that this choice is destructive. In less extreme cases, we can numb ourselves with too much television, mindless eating, Internet surfing, shopping, or other compulsive time wasters. Whatever our "drug" of choice, living a chronically anesthetized life is not taking full advantage of our humanity.

Emotions aren't so scary once we have an outlet for them. Even if you don't yet feel connected to your emotions, you may come closer to feeling, identifying, and understanding them through exercises in creative expression. I think of emotions as pressure building up under a volcano. There are two major kinds of volcanoes. Shield volcanoes, like those that formed the Hawaiian Islands, have accessible outlets where lava can flow freely. While the eruptions can be spectacular, and even explosive at times, their output is productive. Over time that outflow has created something truly magnificent, the highest mountains on earth. Mauna Loa volcano, which forms the Big Island of Hawaii, is taller from its base on the sea floor to its summit than Mount Everest.

The second kind of volcano is like Mount Saint Helens in Washington State. In the volcano's dramatic awakening in 1980, pressure gathered with few safe pathways for release, creating a huge bulge that built up over several weeks. When it reached its breaking point, burning gas, smoke, and ash blew away the side of the mountain in a cataclysmic eruption that left a huge swath of destruction in its path.

No one wants to unleash Mount Saint Helens on her family. One alternative to numbness followed by explosion is to become involved in creative and expressive activities that pioneer safe outlets for our full range of emotions, so that we can release them constructively, rather than destructively. I believe that we are all artists in our own way, and that the need to create and dream is an essential human process that we all deserve to explore.

While thinking of volcanoes and expression, I was continually reminded of Langston Hughes's poem "What Happens to a Dream Deferred?"

What happens to a dream deferred?
Does it dry up
Like a raisin in the sun?
Or fester like a sore—
And then run?
Does it stink like rotten meat?
Or crust and sugar over—
Like a syrupy sweet?
Maybe it just sags
Like a heavy load.
Or does it explode?

The Danger Zone

Sometimes the demands of motherhood pile up until they are almost too much to bear. Anger and frustration escalate until we find ourselves on the verge of losing control, falling into despair, or wondering how we will make it through even the next five minutes. Whether you are confronted with a sick infant or a manipulative six-year-old (or sixteen-year-old), children demand attention, and caring for them can be physically and emotionally draining. That is why it is so important for us to take care of ourselves, to store up reserves to get us through the tough moments. Experienced Moms say that it is worth developing these skills as soon as possible, because they can be used for many aspects of child rearing, including living with teenagers.

Psychotherapist Sarah Cameron has the following recommendations to help Moms cope with that feeling of being on the verge of losing control, which I call "the danger zone."

- Be aware of the warning signs of "HALT." Being hungry, angry, lonely, or tired makes us more vulnerable to entering the danger zone. Unfortunately, HALT elements tend to come with motherhood, especially during the early months, which is why it is essential that we make self-care, sleep, healthy emotional outlets, and nurturing connections with friends important priorities. (HALT originated with twelve-step programs, but Sarah Cameron has adapted the concept to fit her classes for professionals who struggle with emotional sensitivity, and uses this framework with stressed-out parents as well.)

- If you do find yourself in the danger zone, don't make any major decisions right then and there. Don't give any one thought too much power. Decide to push a disturbing thought out of the way for twelve to twenty-four hours, then reevaluate the thought objectively once you are out of crisis mode.

- Seek support from friends, your partner, or a competent therapist or support group. Ask for help with child care, if possible, while you work through an immediate crisis. On more than one occasion, when I've been on my own with my child and have found myself entering the danger zone, I have given *myself* a five-minute time-out alone in my bedroom in order to recenter myself and gather my composure.

Jump-starting Your Creativity

Even if our creative selves have lain dormant for years, becoming a mother can actually help jump-start the creative process. Rediscovering the freedom and joy of children's play is truly one of the gifts of motherhood. My daughter and I play games, improvise songs, and act out stories. I used to be embarrassed by my singing voice. It wasn't all that bad, but I had no confidence in it, and I never wanted anyone to hear it. After years of singing to and with my daughter, I now sing in the shower and along with songs in the car. I belt out show tunes around the house with the enthusiasm of a Broadway veteran. My voice has improved a bit by using it, but what has really changed is that I want to sing, and I don't mind if anyone hears me.

My creative life renewed itself through playing imaginative games with my daughter, and the gift of children's play has reopened creative options that I thought were shut off forever. Way back in junior high, most of us had to choose between playing an instrument and joining the choir, athletics and drama; and art became a graded subject. I pigeonholed myself as a flute-playing "brain" who would do whatever the art teacher said we needed to do to get an A. Other creative out-lets fell by the wayside. It took becoming a Mom to show me that I did not have to accept the limitations I had put on myself, to open me up to the possibility of literally finding my own voice.

Creative activities are a worthy investment of your most precious commodity: time. Signing up for a class can be a good way to carve out an artistic niche. It is always valuable to have the guidance of a talented teacher, but an additional value of signing up for a class is that it solidifies your commitment to the activity. By the time you've registered for the class, paid your fees, put it on the calendar, and negotiated child care, you are likely to stick to your commitment to attend. Sadly, we often find ourselves pushing our own activities aside to accommodate the inevitable creeping demands of our families and the rest of the world. I find that to write, not only do I have to make a date on my calendar, but I often have to get out of the house to really concentrate. Even if I am home alone, the distractions of e-mail, the phone, the mail, and undone housework staring me in the face can be hard to ignore. By working in a coffeehouse or public library, I can enter my creative mental world knowing that there is nothing else I "should" be doing at the moment. You will have to ask for the time to pursue creative activities, and advocate for the importance of that time. It is unlikely that anyone will offer this precious "free" time to you if you do not insist on making it a priority.

While I will always advocate that each Mom will benefit from finding an artistic outlet that is all her own, it is also fun to get your whole family involved whenever possible. If your kids are interested in singing or playing an instrument, can you join in and form a family band? (Watch out, Partridges!) Can you do arts and crafts together, working on the same project, or in parallel? Isn't it sad that we encourage kids to get involved in art, drama, and music, and then provide so few opportunities for adults to continue these interests? My husband and daughter are budding songwriters, and I am a master of the improvised lullaby. My daughter and husband sing and record their songs together on his computer, and I have even dusted off my long-neglected flute to have the chance to play along. We won't be embarking on a world tour anytime soon, but I love that we are creating music together, making recordings that will become unique family mementos.

❋ Inspiration from Your Mojo Sisters

If you are craving a Moms' night out that goes beyond the usual wine-and-appetizers gathering, it can be really fun to get together to brainstorm ideas for expanding your creative lives. Here is one way to facilitate that discussion: Write the headings "Past," "Present," and "Future" on three large sheets of paper, and hang them on a wall. Have each participant fill in the creative activities she has done in the past, what she does now, and what she'd like to try in the future.

The group's list may give you inspiration for new things to try. You may even find a kindred spirit to take a class with you, or someone who is willing to swap child care to help you both carve out time for creative activities.

As a group, you can celebrate your past accomplishments, brainstorm ways to get beyond any present obstacles, and honor your future goals. If you are faced with a short list of "Present" creative outlets, help one another come up with ideas for how to make your future dreams part of your present reality. What do you truly want to add to your life, and what else can you subtract to make time for your essential creative activities? Generate a list of opportunities to create time. You can ask each person to come up with a few "less, more" suggestions, for example, "Less cooking, more painting." Eating leftovers or take-out food one additional evening per week instead of cooking a full meal may give you the time you need to take an art class.

There is a whole universe of creative endeavors from which to choose. To get you started, I have included a list of broad categories to consider, with some activities in each category—but what matters is what appeals to you. Some of these ideas are artistic activities; all are potential opportunities to explore your true feelings and let them out. This collection of ideas is not intended to be a to-do list or a scorecard. If you are stuck or feel totally uncreative, the list may give you an idea for a starting point. Introducing just one creative activity into your life can make a major difference.

FINDING YOUR VOICE
Singing: in any venue, from the shower to the stage.
Public speaking.
Reading out loud: library group, school, or worship service liturgist.
Writing: keep a journal, create poems, write a book.

Write a "life résumé" highlighting all your accomplishments and listing what is important to you, without caring what anyone else would think. Post it where you can see it each day.

Yelling: in a martial arts or self-defense class, alone in the car, group roar with your kids to let off steam.

Negotiating: with your partner, kids, at work. Make your needs known.

Vocalize your emotions: laugh, cry, howl like a dog, roar like a lion. You can practice this with your kids or alone. Remember to breathe!

Drama: act in a play. Take acting lessons or an improvisational acting class. You will probably be familiar with many improv warm-ups, which are often based on silly games you already play with your kids.

VISUAL EXPRESSION

Visit a museum.

Try a new art or revive an old interest: painting, photography, ceramics, glass blowing, weaving, sculpture.

Create a visual symbol for yourself. This can be anything from designing your own business cards, or creating a personal symbol or icon, to designing a book cover for your autobiography or a magazine cover for a feature article on *you*. I encourage you to try creating something visual that represents your true self, and your wishes or goals. We are visual creatures, and physical manifestations of your dreams, even if they currently feel like unattainable fantasies, can help bring them into reality.

POLITICAL EXPRESSION AND ISSUE ADVOCACY

The world needs to hear your political opinions. The issues that affect you most may be the ones ignored or opposed by power players and paid lobbyists. There are many ways to become politically involved, from the local neighborhood level to global activism.

Vote.

Put an opinionated bumper sticker on your car.

Send a letter or e-mail to one of your government representatives.

Volunteer for a political campaign, advocacy group, or event.

Send money to a cause you support.

Write a letter to the editor.

Attend a march or event.

Host a discussion group or community meeting.

Learn about your local and national representatives.

Attend a school board meeting or a town council meeting.

Read the newspaper.

Send a thank-you letter of recognition to someone you admire in your community.

Read a political publication that you do not agree with.

Invite an issue-oriented speaker to present to a group you belong to.

Put a political sign in your yard.

Volunteer at your local voting precinct on Election Day.

Speak to a group about an issue you care about.

Get involved in community radio.

Run for political office.

PHYSICAL EXPRESSION

Dance.

Exercise.

Get a massage.

Join a sports team.

Learn a martial art or take a self-defense class. Explore your untapped power.

Rest and get enough sleep. You can't dream if you don't sleep!

Sex: Communicate with your partner and talk about something you would (or would not) like to do. Try something new: a new position, clothes, or toys. Claim your own experience of sexuality, without worrying about whether you have an orgasm on any given day. Read a sex book. Whisk your partner away for a romantic getaway, even if it's only one night away at a hotel in your own town.

Work

Your career can perform a number of functions in your life, from a necessary task that allows you to pay the bills to a calling that expresses your deepest values. Wherever you are right now, look for opportunities to make the work you already do reflect your personality, beliefs, and priorities. If you don't love your job, there may be ways to increase the agreement between your work and personal lives to maximize your enjoyment. Even if you have a satisfying career, it is important to keep developing an internal sense of identity that is independent of any specific job. Women hold an average of more than eleven jobs in their lifetimes. If you have to reinvent yourself in a new career, it is help-

The Austin Powers Kind of Mojo

Sex is an important element of mojo, or, put another way, mojo is an important part of sex. When Mike Myers was asked to explain shagadelic superspy Austin Powers's use of the word mojo, he didn't define it as sex, as you might expect, but rather as "essence." He's on to something. Mojo is the energy and magic that makes sex come alive, rather than being just another mechanical act.

Once the physical aspects of "sex after the baby arrives" are mastered (healing, foreplay, and lubrication), I encourage you to explore the emotional and spiritual aspects of lovemaking. Sex is an important form of expression and communion between yourself and your partner. With time pressures that keep busy couples apart, a rewarding sex life can provide some of the best moments of connection and renewed intimacy. Becoming a mother can alter our perception of ourselves as sexual beings, and presents us with the challenge and opportunity to continue to develop as sexual beings.

In the United States, our right to sexual expression and exploration is under attack culturally and legally. Even the most traditional couples can find themselves caught in a double bind of being expected to remain happily married to the same person for the next half century, but punished for exploring ways to keep their monogamous sexuality exciting and rewarding. In October 2003, Joanne Webb, a Christian, Republican mother of three was arrested and charged under the Texas obscenity law for her work marketing adult products and sex toys. Joanne is a consultant for Passion Parties, a home-based party business that sells lotions, books, and toys designed to spice up a couple's relationship. She was caught in an undercover sting by narcotics officers posing as a married couple who bought a vibrator and asked for advice on improving their sex life. While charges were

ultimately dismissed, Joanne and her husband had to declare bank-
ruptcy as a result of fighting the legal charges that threatened her with
a year in jail and a $4,000 fine. The real kicker is that it is legal to
own sex toys in Texas, but Joanne violated the law by *explaining how
to use them*. Looks like we still live in an era in which law enforcement
feels comfortable stepping in to silence sex educators, reinforcing the
age-old stereotype that wives are expected to provide sex on demand
but are prohibited from actually enjoying it.

It is up to us to push back against these restrictions. Joanne
Webb has bravely continued to fight to overturn the obscenity laws
that make it a crime to talk about sex.

A group of my Mom friends gathered for a similar "Temptations
Party" a while back, and while we started out feeling embarrassed,
it was fun to overcome those inhibitions, learn something new, and
have an open discussion about sexuality. The home-based parties
are an interesting option for women who would never set foot in
a store that sells erotic products. The consultant's presentation was
focused on education and fun. Our party was a girls' night out
because none of us were comfortable having this conversation in
a mixed gender setting, but the overwhelming report was that our
husbands were all for it!

ful to have a centered starting point, a sense of who you are outside
your role as mother or employee, that can guide you as you start over
in a new field. Through friends, activities, or just spending ten quiet
minutes meditating every day, it's important to maintain a sliver of
your identity that is recognizable as the essential *you*—an authentic
sense of self that is deeply embedded, portable, and relaunchable, no
matter what external realities come your way.

❈ Mothering Is Creating

Motherhood is literally the ultimate creative act. No matter how many times we replay the births of our children in our minds, the moment of introducing a new human being into the world never ceases to be a miracle. Anthropologist Angeles Arrien affirms the connection between motherhood and creativity with her description of one of my favorite symbols, the Tarot card the Princess of Disks, which represents creativity and birth of new forms:

> *The Princess of Disks is the pregnant lady who represents mastery of creative power. She is a woman who has been over the volcano and through the briar patch. She bears new life that has been gestating and incubating within her for some time. She is fertile and abundant with either a new identity, life style, creative project, or human being. Her pioneer nature is represented by her Aries crown. The snake on her shoulder, which transforms into an ermine cloak, represents her earthly and ancient passion to create.*
>
> *The Princess of Disks desires to give birth to new forms that are in alignment with who she is. She is determined to manifest harvest in a balanced and organic way. She approaches motherhood issues or issues surrounding her own mother in creative ways.* (Arrien, The Tarot Handbook, *p. 143*)

I can't think of a better description of what it means to be a Mojo Mom, a woman who has allowed the transformative experience of motherhood to bring new forms of creativity and power to all areas of her life. The Princess of Disks does not gloss over the challenges of motherhood but instead uses everything she has experienced to fuel her creative fire. Mojo is energy, and the scientist in me heartily

Princess of Disks

believes that like other forms of energy, mojo that arises in one form can be transformed and redirected into another. The sun's energy is released as heat and light, which can be changed into electricity by a solar cell, captured by plants and stored as food energy, or transformed by chemical reactions into signals that burn images onto film or our eyes' own retinas. Mojo can originate as a positive burst of energy, as inspiration, or as a chafe, an itch, a hungering need. Mojo

rises through artistic expression, allowing us to experience our feelings, relax in a silent moment, or in a million other ways—from the
simplicity of enjoying a quiet meal to the exhilaration of playing in
a symphony. Mojo is the energy that recharges our bodies, renews
our spirits, and exercises our minds. When we make it a priority to
nurture our creative energies, we reconnect with our deepest selves.
When this connection is combined with an awareness of the larger
world, and an exploration of the values and ideas that are most important to us, we are able to move forward to manifest our beliefs as reality. What begins as play may evolve into directed action, answering
the question, *What is my unique contribution to the world?* The world
desperately needs the leadership of women and mothers, as actors in
the public sphere. We will continue to move forward toward action as
our exploration of mojo continues.

References and Resources

Creative Exploration

Check local listings for classes in your area offered by community colleges,
university continuing education programs, local arts centers, recreation de-
partments, or private classes listed online or in your telephone directory.

The Artist's Way: A Spiritual Path to Higher Creativity by Julia Cameron

Julia Cameron presents a comprehensive plan for becoming an "unblocked
creative," complete with a map telling you how to begin your journey, daily activities, and strategies to overcome roadblocks you may encounter on your way.

The Creative Habit—Learn It and Use It For Life by Twyla Tharp

Renowned as a dancer and choreographer, Twyla Tharp tells her readers that "in order to be creative, you have to know how to prepare to be creative"— and then she teaches them how to do it. This is an excellent resource that features exercises that will inspire any artist, novice or expert, in any field.

The Tarot Handbook: Practical Applications of Ancient Visual Symbols by Angeles Arrien, Ph.D.

Angeles Arrien views symbols as "the creative ideas that function as a universal language in that area where an individual's internal and external worlds intersect and attempt to dialogue with one another" (p. 12). Her work has reclaimed the Tarot from the limited context of fortune-telling to explain its use as a symbolic system that can be used as a validation, rather than a substitute, for one's own intuitive process.

The Art of Possibility: Transforming Professional and Personal Life by Rosamund Stone Zander and Benjamin Zander

If you are feeling limited by your role as a mother, *The Art of Possibility* will help you see life from many new angles and may lead you to new paths that help you reach your goals.

101 Improv Games for Children and Adults by Bob Bedore

This is a great book for any family to read together, because it features games that work for kids and adults. With older kids, your family could throw an all-ages improv party. Some games require breaking into teams, which provides an opportunity to have "kids versus adults" play in a noncompetitive, fun setting.

Women's Voices in Public Discourse

BlogHer
www.BlogHer.com

Women's writing has exploded in this new era of online citizen journalism. There are far too many talented bloggers to list individually, but I can tell you that the BlogHer community is a great place to find a treasure trove of quality writing.

Women's e-News
www.WomensENews.org

Women's e-News is the only news service that is devoted to daily coverage of the issues affecting women's lives.

The Op-Ed Project
www.TheOpEdProject.org

Writer Catherine Orenstein leads seminars that teach women how to raise their voices by publishing opinion pieces.

Sexuality

Great Sex for Moms: Ten Steps to Nurturing Passion While Raising Kids by Valerie Davis Raskin, M.D.

Raskin diagnoses the common obstacles to great sex and provides thoughtful resources and prescriptions to awaken a sleepy libido—now, rather than waiting until your kids leave for college! Her advice is comprehensive, and she includes a chapter for Dads.

Sexy Mamas: Keeping Your Sex Life Alive While Raising Kids by Cathy Winks and Anne Semans

Written with optimism and wit by women who work at San Francisco's woman-positive sex shop Good Vibrations, *Sexy Mamas* features a great discussion on negotiating parenting roles with your partner as an essential foundation for building your sexual relationship.

Sexy Mamas also references my favorite factoid of all time. In the late nineteenth century, the vibrator was "the fifth home appliance to be electrified, following the sewing machine, fan, teakettle, and toaster, but preceding the vacuum cleaner or steam iron" (p. 143). Now, that's a refreshing list of priorities!

Mating in Captivity: Unlocking Erotic Intelligence by Esther Perel

Couples therapist Perel takes on the paradoxical union of committed relationships and sexual desire, and explains what it takes to bring lust home.

Sex Smart: How Your Childhood Shaped Your Sexual Life and What to Do About It by Aline P. Zoldbrod, Ph.D.

Zoldbrod's workbook guides each reader through an understanding of childhood socialization and how it affects adult sexual life. Body image, power dynamics, gender roles, and adolescence are covered in depth. Parents will benefit from reading *Sex Smart* to understand all the ways we influence the development of our children's sexual attitudes and beliefs. This book is a powerful tool for all of us, whether we came from loving or conflicted backgrounds. Zoldbrod advises that people who have experienced sexual abuse would benefit from reading this book with a therapist's guidance.

Resurrecting Sex: Resolving Sexual Problems and Rejuvenating Your Relationship by David Schnarch, Ph.D.

Written by a sex therapist, *Resurrecting Sex* is a valuable resource for couples who are experiencing sexual difficulties.

CHAPTER 7

Daddies as Mojo Partners

When Mama ain't happy, ain't nobody happy.
—MOM'S WISDOM

In business as in life, you don't get what you deserve,
you get what you negotiate.
—MASTER NEGOTIATOR CHESTER KARRASS

As each of us works to untangle the knotty issues connecting identity, family, and career, the relationship between life partners is an important focal point to examine.

I happily acknowledge that families come in many forms and arrangements. This chapter will focus on the relationship between mothers and fathers, because gender roles and assumptions tend to come to the forefront when a baby enters the picture. "Traditional" roles and their cultural underpinnings will impact a woman's life whether she is single, partnered, or married, with a co-parent of either gender. Unfortunately, motherhood is still a key trigger for gender stereotyping at home and in the workplace.

New mothers may be dismayed to learn the extent to which parenthood marks the front lines of gender disparity for our generation.

Women have gained so many opportunities in the past few decades that it is easy to feel complacent, tempting to think that the major battles of 1970s feminism have been won and that we've achieved equal status.

Then one day perhaps your boyfriend makes the leap to husband, and maybe it's still so far, so good. You are both working on your own careers and feel confident that you are developing an equal relationship.

But when baby makes three, gender roles pop up with surprising speed and vigor. Many of us have created relationships that feel progressive and egalitarian, but we can't escape the fact that hidden fault lines of gender inequality run right through the foundation of our society. Adding a baby to the family brings these issues to the surface. A couple's formerly parallel lives may reach a fork in the road that branches off in two radically different directions marked "Mom" and "Dad." A lack of family-friendly policies creates pressure that pushes men to specialize in employment and women to specialize in child care. Seemingly small divergences that arise at the birth of a child can translate into significantly different life paths for women and men. Author Rachel Cusk says that "childbirth and motherhood are the anvil on which sexual inequality was forged, and the women in our society whose responsibilities, expectations, and experience are like those of men are right to approach it with trepidation" (*A Life's Work*, p. 8).

While each couple's situation will be different, there are things we can do to prepare to share parenting, and strategies that will help us recover if the sharing dynamic gets too far out of balance. Ideally, couples will enter into parenthood with an awareness of these issues and a set of tools to use to create a fair and satisfying partnership. Men are a key part of this equation, but for better or worse, women really need to pay attention to the couple's developing roles as parents. We are caught in a half-changed world that does not provide any easy solutions for women. If the process is left on cultural autopilot, a mother is likely to find that she is automatically assigned the roles of primary caregiver and household manager—doing those tasks herself or arranging and managing qualified paid caregivers—no matter what other responsibilities she has taken on.

A More Perfect Union

The good news is that we've reached the point where we really understand that men make excellent parents, and it is possible to develop an equitable partnership. To create a more perfect union, women need to develop two complementary and equally important sets of skills: collaboration and negotiation. Collaboration develops a satisfying partnership between two actively involved, appreciated parents who share common values and goals. On the flip side, you need to make your needs known, and negotiation is an absolutely necessary skill to be able to strike fair deals with your partner.

Ideally, it helps to start thinking of these issues early on. If you know yourself and your partner, and talk about your values and child-rearing philosophy before you commit to a life together, you'll be in a stronger position to state what you want. In reality, it's pretty typical for individuals to discover their own beliefs, not to mention their partner's, as they go along. Wherever you are at this moment, it's not too late to start reshaping your relationship by developing new common ground.

My guiding principle is that parents should strive to build an *equitable* partnership. No two families will have exactly the same power-sharing arrangement, but the underlying principle of equity means that both parents feel that they are getting a fair deal, and that their personal needs as well as the family's needs are being met. Couples will share parenting responsibilities or specialize to different degrees, but a foundation of respect and goodwill, an ongoing willingness to negotiate, and a goal to create equity will help keep the family on track.

❋ Avoiding the Mommy Trap

Julie Shields's excellent book *How to Avoid the Mommy Trap* focuses on strategies that facilitate the process of truly shared parenting. The "mommy trap" is the result of the social forces that pull women and men apart along traditional gender lines. Shields defines the mommy trap as ensnaring a mother whenever:

- She takes on parenting or household responsibilities that result in more unpaid work, and less leisure and personal time than she would like, particularly in comparison with her husband;
- She does nothing to change the situation beyond expressing anger, complaint, and resignation;
- Inherited preconceptions—including those about what men and women can and should do, how child and household care should be performed, and that the universe of work and child-care arrangements is rigidly predetermined—prevent her and her family from finding a solution to their problem (Shields, *How to Avoid the Mommy Trap*, pp. 13–14).

Those are the major challenges of modern parenthood in a nutshell. One of the strategies for avoiding the mommy trap is to encourage men to develop their own parenting skills. This means that at the very least, fathers should be encouraged to spend time alone with their children so that they develop into fully qualified caregivers. Dads are not doing Moms a *favor,* and they are not *babysitting* when they care for their own children.

The Four-Thirds Solution

The Four-Thirds Solution is a strategy that helps couples pursue equally shared parenting. Child development expert Stanley Greenburg calculates that two parents can expect to be able to fill the equivalent of one and one-third full-time jobs (about fifty-five hours a week) before they need to rely heavily on supplemental paid child care.

Developing a Satisfying Partnership

Moms can consciously step back and invite participation from their partners. Writer and negotiation expert Rhona Mahony says that mothers should think about creating "affirmative action" opportunities for Dads. Sociologists have found that birth mothers enter motherhood with a head start in their attachment to their babies resulting from the nine-month commitment of pregnancy. Birth mothers arrive at their baby's birth with an established physical connection with the child, and have already had nine months of practice in altering their priorities, schedules, and bodies to accommodate the baby's needs. Men need extra primary caregiving opportunities to develop their parenting expertise and attachment. In dual-earner couples, even a few weeks of maternity leave can intensify the head-start effect, so it is important that couples consciously establish sustainable patterns of sharing parenting and household duties. Even though the early months with a newborn represent an exceptional time in a family's life, it can be helpful to keep this saying in mind: *Begin as you wish to continue.* At the very least, get on a long-term sustainable path as soon as possible.

✳ Negotiating a Fair Division of Labor

Discussions of household work can get highly politicized. I am not going to tell you who has to do what job. I strongly believe that attempts to keep score and rigidly divide the work into *literally equal* halves are doomed to fail. (This is the surest route to becoming competitors rather than collaborators.) A more realistic goal is to strive to negotiate an *equitable* division of labor. This would be a plan that both of you can live with, a plan that requires ongoing participation and renegotiation to adapt to the changes that all of you will experience as your family grows up. Everyone in the family needs to participate in the household as much as they possibly can. Teach your children to do all that they can for themselves as they develop, so that they don't expect to be catered to their whole lives.

Here are some general principles of housework for both parents to keep in mind:

- Tackle each chore from its logical starting point to its conclusion.

    One of a woman's most common complaints is that her husband is ambitious and creative at work but won't initiate any housework unless asked to, and then will take her requests extremely literally. For example, if a wife asks her husband to take out the trash, he will dutifully drag the cans to the curb, but he might not think to empty the household wastebaskets into the cans first. Moms often spend all day chasing down the endless links in the chain of household tasks. If a Dad, on his own, changed a dirty diaper, gave the baby a bath and changed her outfit, took the full diaper pail bag out to the garage, and took the cans to the curb, many a Mom would be eternally grateful, and feel validated that she was working with an involved co-parent.

- At the same time, think about how the workflow of chores you initiate affects your partner.

  Following your work to its logical conclusion, or asking your partner if this is a good time to enlist help, is always appreciated. For example, if your housework agreement says (formally or informally) that you wash the laundry and your partner folds it and puts it away, it would be really helpful if you would make sure that you started a laundry project at a good time for both of you. Your partner will not appreciate coming to bed at midnight to find three loads of unfolded laundry piled high, standing in the way of her night's sleep.

- Hire outside help if you can afford it and want it.

  I highly recommend hiring a cleaning service to help out with the big chores. This does not lift the entire housework burden, but it helps make it manageable. I have found that I spend the same amount of time on housework whether I have a cleaning service or not, but with the addition of out-side help, the results are much better! The house is actually picked up one day a week, the dog's fur balls don't have a chance to grow into full-fledged tumbleweeds, and the bath-rooms are always clean.

  I purposefully subscribe to realistic, imperfect standards

of household order, and fortunately my husband and I are on a similar wavelength. Aspiring to an impressive level of domesticity is not on my agenda. I have enough hours in the day to have an immaculate house, or a messy-but-sanitary house and a completed book. Here is the book. Call first if you are coming over to visit the house.

- Give up control to get equity.

As you begin to divide family responsibilities, remember that if you criticize the way your partner does a task, you may as well be claiming that task for yourself. It is to your advantage to become an expert in power sharing. If you treat your husband as though he's an incompetent boob with the baby, then he is likely to pull away from that responsibility. Julie Shields points out that this is a major sticking point for many women. On the one hand, we want men to participate in child rearing; on the other hand, part of us still clings to the traditional view that mothers really do it better. This mindset needs to change. Fathers may do things differently, but resist the temptation to view this as "the wrong way." Fathers bring their own brand of play and leadership into the family. We mothers have to learn to give up control to get equity at home.

Mothers have a reason to be pickier about their household standards because they know they are the ones who are more likely to get criticized if their kids show up at church wearing pajamas, if family thank-you notes don't get written, or if the house is a mess. However, in the long run it is worth cultivating a more forgiving standard of parenting and housekeeping. For one thing, if we do it all and make it look effortless, we are not going to get any help from our families.

How can we avoid this particular trap? It is essential to make the invisible work visible, and then divide it fairly. I try to involve my husband and daughter as much as possible in household chores, and do housework when the whole family is together. It is well worth the investment of time and energy to train your kids to become involved from a young age. To little kids, work is play. It can take longer to do chores with them, but in the long run the effort pays off with capable children who grow into competent adults. Start this process when they are very young, and remember to add new responsibilities as the kids get older. Even an eight-year-old can be taught to manage his own laundry—there is no excuse for sending a kid off to college not knowing how to take care of him- or herself.

When Couples Don't Share

The huge task of managing the invisible work of family life can lead to resentment when Mom is expected to keep it all together for the whole family unit. On a bad day, she may feel like an unappreciated servant whose brain has been taken over by family requests: "Mommy, where's Barbie's other shoe?" "Honey, do we have any wrapping paper?" "Mom, where's my homework?"

This dynamic can become particularly irritating when the other adult in the house can't be bothered to keep track of what is going on in family life. Women have different levels of tolerance for conflicts revolving around fairness and participation in family responsibilities. I have seen plenty of marriages break up over these issues, so I always take them seriously. This reader comment posted on Tara Parker-Pope's *New York Times* Well blog describes one woman's rising anger about the imbalance in her family:

Is Your Suitcase Packed?

The work that mothers are stereotypically expected to do involves more than just chores around the house. It's the mental planning and tracking required to keep the invisible three-ring circus of family life running in the background all the time. Here's a scene from my life that many mothers have told me that they relate to:

"Is your suitcase packed?" asked Michael, innocuously but expectantly. My husband, our daughter, and I would be leaving for my family's reunion in three days, and his small red duffel bag was already organized and packed, ready to go. My huge suitcase was still hidden in the back of our closet. Michael didn't make a big deal about the fact that he was ready and I wasn't, but I thought I could sense a hint of "There she goes again, always waiting until the last minute to get her act together." It's true that I'm always about fifteen minutes behind schedule getting out of the house on vacation day. I am also likely to stop the car and run back for "just one more thing" as we pull out of the driveway. But let's look at what leads up to the point where the car pulls away.

Michael's vacation preparations required him to wrap up his work at the office, and then at home he did a little laundry, picked out books to take along, and packed his own suitcase. This was easily accomplished three days before our departure.

My preparations started months before, when I coordinated the itinerary with our extended family. I bought the plane tickets and picked them up. The week before we left, I went into full vacation-prep mode. Taking care of the dog and cat alone involved more than a dozen steps, from making plans for their care to getting the required immunizations at the vet to buying their supplies.

Then there were the tasks involved with getting our daughter ready to go. In addition to doing her laundry and setting aside an extra change of clothes for the airplane carry-on, I shopped for snacks and activities to entertain us on the nine-hour journey, and bought a present for her cousin who would have a birthday party at the reunion.

The list of mundane but essential household jobs went on. I sent an e-mail to stop the newspaper, helped my Mom get her house closed up for the trip, deposited checks and paid bills, cleaned out the refrigerator, and took out the trash. The evening before the trip, I set out clothes for our daughter to change into at the airport, since we'd get up early and take her wearing her pajamas. Then I finally packed her clothes and mine into our shared suitcase and collapsed into bed after midnight.

The morning of our six thirty A.M. departure, I unplugged the computers, left on some strategically placed lights and turned off the rest, and thought about what I must have forgotten. I sent my family out to the car while I packed milk and cold snacks into our carry-on, locked the doors, and checked them (twice). As we drove out of the neighborhood, we stopped to deposit a stack of mail into the mailbox. We were on our way.

Event planner and ringmaster all in one. Is your suitcase packed?

To your question [about responsibility sharing between husbands and wives]:

I'm the female half of my hetero marriage. My day starts at least an hour prior to my husband getting out of bed. During this time I change our toddler, feed her breakfast, clean up the kitchen, possibly start a load of laundry, and get myself dressed and ready for work. Sometimes I feed myself and start coffee for myself and DH.

DH usually handles lunch, consisting either of leftovers of a dinner I made previously, or takeout sandwiches.

My workday usually ends, or is interrupted, when it is time to make dinner. DH picks this up maybe 1 or 2 times a week, and there is a strong chance the meal will be takeout if he is cooking. Budget and nutrition concerns abound.

My weekends generally include picking up the house and vacuuming the entire place, cleaning up dog messes in the backyard, planning meals for the coming week and getting the groceries (often accompanied by DH).

I'm the principal source of child care and activities for our toddler on the weekend and in the evenings. I'm the only one who notices the bathrooms need cleaning. I seem to be the only one who remembers that Friday is trash day. I'm also the one who does the taxes, pays the bills as they come in, and makes sure our checking account isn't going to go overdraft. I'm also the one managing questions and decisions about renovations being made to two rental properties.

You might think this is all a function of my income being lower than DH's and thus, my time being the more worthy choice for exploitation for "unpaid" labor. That's not the case, however: for over 18 months I've been [the] sole income, and prior to that, my income was the same or higher than DH's.

It's not a healthy situation.

All I really want for my birthday is a little more initiative and contribution on my DH's part to recognize the work that goes into keeping our household running. I don't want to nag or make him "honey-do" lists, I want him to SEE what needs to be done, and do it.

—Posted by Helen

Tara Parker-Pope's response:

It didn't surprise [me]. I was interested in the statement that a lot of women have a lot of simmering anger because they feel like they have to do everything. I think a lot of men are clueless about how angry their wives are about this perceived imbalance of responsibility. (Well blog, The New York Times, June 10, 2008)

Once a couple becomes this disconnected, they will desperately need remedial communication and negotiation, perhaps facilitated by a marriage counselor, to get things back on track. It's a battle worth fighting, because no one looks forward to a life dominated by seething resentment bubbling below the surface of their relationship.

Who Are We Now That We Are Mom and Dad?

The intense newborn phase has a way of erasing the memories of our lives before becoming Moms, and I believe it is crucial to remember who we were, and to explore all facets of who we are now, as well as who we hope to become. Successfully navigating this new territory requires couples to find ways to stay connected while grappling with their new roles as Mom and Dad. As novelist Nora Ephron memorably said, "A child is a grenade. When you have a baby, you set off an explosion in your marriage, and when the dust settles, your marriage is different than what it was. Not better, necessarily; not worse, necessarily; but different" (Ephron, *Heartburn*, as quoted in Gottman, *The Seven Principles for Making Marriage Work*, p. 211).

Psychologist John Gottman has learned a great deal about the dangers and opportunities inherent in relationships as he has studied thousands of couples over the past thirty years. His advice is based on extensive observational research, not just his opinion or conventional wisdom held by marital therapists. I highly recommend his readable, practical book, *The Seven Principles for Making Marriage Work*.

The birth of a first child is a joyous event, but the fact is that it also puts a great deal of strain on adult relationships. In the year after a first baby arrives, 70 percent of wives experience a precipitous drop in their marital satisfaction (Gottman, *Seven Principles,* p. 211). In other words, it is a myth that having a baby will automatically "bring you closer together." With childbirth, we are again faced with crisis, containing the elements of both danger and opportunity. The addition of children to your relationship is a challenge. Successfully negotiating that challenge together can be one of the most rewarding experiences of your life.

Gottman has investigated both the reasons that two-thirds of new mothers feel miserable, and the clues to why the remaining third sail through the transition unscathed. His findings resonate strongly with the core concepts of *Mojo Mom*—he validates the idea that the transition to motherhood causes a profound metamorphosis and reorientation of meaning in a woman's life. Men have much more choice about whether and how much their lives will change after becoming fathers. Gottman concludes that the key to maintaining a happy relationship is for the new father to stay connected with his wife, experiencing this transformation with her. Valued aspects of a couple's "old life" together may be put on hold for now, but both partners can work together to create new activities together and shared meaning around their growing family. Marriage and family are not opposed; they can be integrated. You need time together to continue to turn toward each other. On the one hand, it is important to get away for dinner as a couple, Gottman says, but on the other hand, it is fine if you find yourselves talking about the baby during your date. Partners stay connected when they make the philosophical shift to parenthood together (Gottman, *Seven Principles,* pp. 212–213).

✳ The Can Opener of Love

The presumption of goodwill, affection, and respect between partners is essential for a strong relationship. These feelings must be carefully tended. Nurturing our daily, loving interactions is more important than making grand romantic overtures. When our daughter asked, "Mommy, how did you know you wanted to marry Daddy?" my first reaction was to say, "Because he gave me a can opener." Back when we were dating, he noticed that I had a poorly designed manual can opener that barely worked. One of the first gifts he ever gave me was a Swiss-engineered can opener that did work—not just any can opener, but his own. He couldn't find a new opener that worked as well as his, so he gave me his even though he knew it would be hard to find another one just like it. It wasn't roses or diamonds, but more than a decade later, every time I use it, this simple gift continues to remind me how much he really cares about me. (And no, I don't worry that he married me just to get the can opener back!)

When children arrive and life instantly becomes more compli-cated and busy, it is essential to work as collaborators, and not be-come adversaries. For new parents, it is particularly important to work together to prevent a buildup of resentment in the wife, which could threaten the goodwill and affection you have created together. Re-sentment can be avoided if the new mother's emotional needs are expressed, heard, respected, and met. This is the foundation of the *Mojo Mom* approach.

Of course, a new father's resentment can create problems too, but the stresses brought on by the transition to motherhood can lead to a particularly noxious type of resentment that reflects the frustration of *both* partners. The fact that women usually end up being the barometers of a relationship's emotional health creates burdens for both women and men. This situation arises from the different socialization that girls and boys experience throughout childhood, particularly the way that only girls are given permission to express emotion. Therapist Terrence Real thoroughly explores the complex relationship connecting socialization, emotion, intimacy, and shutting down, written from a man's perspective. His book *How Can I Get Through to You? Closing the Intimacy Gap Between Men and Women* provides an insightful, challenging look into the forces that shape us as men and women:

> By and large, girls and women are raised in our society to know more about, and want more from, relationships than do most boys and men. I call this the intimacy gap. Most women would make good relational coaches for men. But men tend to find their partner's attempts to "shape them up" controlling and condescending. After a time, most women learn to back off and become passive about how they are treated in relationships— but not without resentment. And that resentment shows up as withdrawal. As women shut down their needs, they also shut down their sense of pleasure. They want less pleasure; they are less interested in pleasing their partners. While there may be much that works wonderfully in the relationship, there is also a sense of chronic resentment, as women feel unheard in their relationships. While men, who are just doing what they've been programmed to do—work hard, try to be more involved in the family, try to be responsible and responsive—feel progressively that they will "never get it right." The result is a resentful, dissatisfied woman matched with an unappreciated and unloved-feeling man. (Real, How Can I Get Through to You?, p. 23)

Getting Away from It All . . . and Being Glad to Come Home

It is really important for both Moms and Dads to have a chance to get away from their daily life. Stay-at-home Moms, in particular, can feel trapped in their daily routines, given that there is no boundary between work and life, and little time to feel "off duty." Stretching the family bonds once in a while gives a Mom a chance to miss her family, and reminds her how dear they are to her—just like the country song says: "How Can I Miss You When You Won't Go Away?"

I recommend three stages in getting away from it all. First, when both parents are ready, find a reliable caregiver for your baby so that you can go away for a romantic overnight or weekend getaway. I do not recommend doing this the first time you resume lovemaking after the baby is born—a big-deal romantic trip could create too much pressure on both of you to perform. But once you have settled into a groove at home with your baby, the time will come when you are ready to get away to reconnect as a couple, not just as parents. Even if you travel only five miles away and stay at a hotel in your town, a romantic dinner and night away from home can feel like a full-fledged vacation. A new setting and time alone are surefire ingredients to rekindle your romance. A full night's sleep is heaven. Even reading the paper over coffee the next morning will feel like a luxury if you haven't had a leisurely breakfast in recent memory.

Second, it can be wonderfully renewing for a new Mom to get away for a weekend with her friends for fun and female bonding. My Moms' group retreats for an annual Moms' Weekend Away. This year, we managed to get twenty-two Moms, whose children ranged from babies to college age, away to the mountains. We had a blast and strengthened our friendships in a way that could be done only by spending an extended amount of time together.

Third, find an opportunity to send Mom away alone for a professional trip. Even if you are not employed, you can find a professional conference, a weekend class in an area of interest, or a volunteer opportunity that calls you away from home for a couple of days. This type of trip serves several vital functions. It gets your brain working and reminds you who you are as a creative or professional person. Leaving Dad at home with the kids will give you *both* an appreciation for all that you do. The "invisible" work of mothering becomes apparent when you have to get someone else to do it. All the things you do every day without thinking—the work that is so unconscious and routine that it does not even make it onto your calendar—is suddenly a long list of tasks to be covered by someone else. By taking on the role of primary caregiver on a regular basis, Dad will be reminded just how much work, juggling, and coordination go into the care of young children, as well as how rewarding it can be.

I believe it is healthy for a Mom to have enough time away from home to miss her kids and partner. Time away renews perspective. When I get away, I realize how much I value my family, and the freedom I have in being able to be at home as much as I need to. I am so excited to see my daughter and husband when I get home. I love the initial rush of freedom that comes with staying in a hotel, but I also realize that business travel is not as glamorous as I imagine it to be. My husband has a very demanding travel schedule. By doing some work-related travel myself, I can empathize with his draining itinerary, rather than just being jealous that he is going to London, Paris, Tokyo, or New York, while I am staying put in Chapel Hill.

The buildup of resentment in a Mom is a key indicator that something needs to be addressed in the relationship, while acknowledging that the underlying dynamic inevitably involves both partners.

❋ Advanced Mojo Support

Once your family's basic survival needs are being met, you can move on to advanced mojo support. You deserve the opportunity to continue developing as a person, not just as a Mom, and to do so you will need support to create time and space for your own grown-up pursuits. You may lose sight of your former self for a while. It is normal to go through this phase when you have a tiny baby at home, but you need to make sure you don't get stuck in limbo, unable to reconnect with yourself. Each woman has a different need for solitude or separateness from her identity as a Mom. Some women feel very fulfilled by the hard work of managing a home and family. Others yearn to develop that part of their selves that is theirs alone, whether that means returning to a career or exploring personal interests.

If both parents work outside the home, it can be even harder to find time to develop personal interests, but it is still essential to do so. It can help to formally build time into your schedule for each of you to have your own personal time. Parent trainer Donna Erickson recommends a "split-family weekend" schedule for busy couples (at least on an occasional basis): on Saturday, the day is divided into a free half-day for Mom while Dad watches the kids, and a free half-day for Dad while Mom watches the kids. Sunday is spent together as a family. Finally, continue to strengthen your connection as a couple by investing in a trusted babysitter or trading off child care with another family to create regular opportunities to spend time together.

Mojo Dad Has His Say

by Michael Tiemann

I did not read a single book about how to be a parent while Amy was pregnant, or if I did I don't remember. I do remember going to parenting class at the local YWCA, and while I did learn a few things about caring for my wife and baby, most of the class was about successfully navigating the modern American health-care system. When I first held our daughter and then handed her to Amy, that's when it hit me: "This is for real." Whatever I lacked in the latest parenting knowledge I would compensate for with cunning, commitment, and love.

When asked to share my Daddy perspective for this book, I came up with six interrelated themes that explain my Daddy Mojo. There might be a few I've missed, and they may not apply to everyone, but they really worked for me.

1. *Why Zebras Don't Get Ulcers* by Robert Sapolsky explains the biological basis of "Hakuna Matata" and makes the case that we humans are simply not designed for long-term stresses like sitting in daily traffic jams or growing up in poverty. Instead, we're built for dealing with short-term stress, like a Zebra outrunning a lion.

As an entrepreneur who started his first business using money that had been set aside for rent, I have seen my share of stress. But I have always separated that which I cannot control from that which I can, and I focus on what I can control. Whatever parenting situation I found myself in, I kept my focus on what I could control, and if there was no way to control the baby's crying, I didn't let it stress me. It might have kept me awake, but it did not stress me.

2. *Puppy training was parent training.* A year before our daughter was born, my wife and I adopted a puppy. According to the breed description, this dog was the last thing we should have brought into our house if we planned to have children, but my wife was convinced that with enough puppy school we could have a happy home with a dog and a child. We were in puppy school for eighteen months.

     Puppy school teaches social behavior—how to take control, how to command respect, how to show affection, how to reward—without the politics. Puppy school is not just about training a dog, but about training oneself to be consistent, set expectations, and follow through. I have never trained our daughter to do tricks, nor have I been a Captain Von Trapp, but the training I received, and applied, from puppy school has meant a lot more fun and a lot less whining when I am with my daughter.

3. *Create the flow, then go with it.* Amy studied aikido, and when she had her first belt test, she invited me to the demonstration. After that I suggested that she use aikido with our puppy (then a seven-pound fuzz ball who was hard to control). With the advice "Don't try to put the dog on its back, just put your hand to the ground and the dog will follow," she mastered a task that had stymied her for six weeks.

     Similarly, I practice directing energy where I want it to go. I don't force my daughter to do things, but I act so that she can simply follow. Whereas conventional parenting wisdom says, "Choose your battles carefully," I choose no battle at all. It is remarkable how much more effective it is to have no battle than even a carefully chosen one.

4. *Play with life's puzzles.* Because I approached parent-hood with so little preparation, I had no choice but to treat the whole experience like a giant puzzle: What does this mean? What does that mean? The challenge of the puzzle is not to mechanically force tab A into slot B. The challenge is to understand what the puzzle is and how it works.

By accepting the puzzle approach, I believe I learned more quickly from my interactions and playful experiments than I ever could have by trying to sift through a thousand different theories to see which one actually applied.

5. *"Be the change you want to see in the world."* Who am I to argue with Mahatma Gandhi's wisdom? When I saw something I didn't like, or didn't see something I really wanted, I always first asked myself, *What can I do about this?*

When I felt that others in our family were leaning too much on the TV to entertain our daughter (and to give themselves time to do something else), I didn't say, "Hey, let's turn off the tube and be a family together." Instead, when it was my turn to be in charge, I found ways of in-volving our daughter in the daily chores that also needed to be done. I made everything a project, and watching TV was just never part of the project. Within a few months, I had demonstrated, without ever saying it, how to avoid TV completely, get the job done, and stay sane. And amaz-ingly enough, we began to notice that our daughter was happier, more helpful, and less whiny on days when she watched no TV compared with days when she watched even thirty minutes of TV.

6. *And in all of the above, practice respect.* Raising a child is not about proving you are right or that another person is wrong. Raising a child is a puzzle, a challenge, a reward,

and it is amazing. Practicing all of the above doesn't mean everything's going to be easy or work perfectly—it's hard work! But when the work gets hard, it makes me respect that much more the work that I never see my wife do while I am not at home. And out of respect, I recommit myself to figuring out how to make my parenting work even better, and what I can do so that next time this energy will work for us, not against us.

And let me just say that while I have no idea how it will happen, I'm sure that I'll be eating all these words when our daughter is a teenager. In the meantime, she's absolutely wonderful, and I feel privileged to be her parent.

Making sure that you continue to develop your own sense of self benefits your relationship and your whole family in the long run. Parenthood may feel like it lasts forever . . . until your children are grown. Then, older parents say, those years may feel like they sped by in a flash. You and your partner may have thirty years or more alone together after your grown-up children have left home. The connections you establish now between the two of you, even during these intense parenting years, will pay off with a mature and involved relationship when it is "just the two of you" again.

✎ REFERENCES AND RESOURCES

How to Avoid the Mommy Trap: A Roadmap for Sharing Parenting and Making It Work by Julie Shields

Practical and eye-opening, this book will change the way you approach motherhood.

The Seven Principles for Making Marriage Work by John Gottman, Ph.D., and Nan Silver

This accessible, research-based guide describes the key factors that help marriages succeed.

How Can I Get Through to You? Closing the Intimacy Gap Between Men and Women by Terrence Real

Real's work can be a challenging read but is a fascinating look at how the differential socialization of girls and boys has long-lasting effects on the ways we relate to one another.

The New Father: A Dad's Guide to the First Year by Armin Brott

Brott's month-by-month guide for Dads as they experience the first year of their child's life is an essential addition to any parenting library.

Equally Shared Parenting Web site
www.EquallySharedParenting.com

Amy and Marc Vachon provide tips and tools for sharing family life more equally. The Vachons view the issue as broader than a black-and-white fifty-fifty split, providing many ideas to allow both parents to purposefully share breadwinning, child raising, housework, and recreation time.

The Bitch in the House: 26 Women Tell the Truth About Sex, Solitude, Work, Motherhood, and Marriage edited by Cathi Hanauer

In this no-holds-barred collection of essays, twenty-six women invite readers into their lives, minds, and bedrooms to talk about the choices they've made, what's working, and what's not.

The Bastard on the Couch: 27 Men Try Really Hard to Explain Their Feelings About Love, Loss, Fatherhood, and Freedom edited by Daniel Jones

In this companion to *The Bitch in the House*, Cathi Hanauer's husband, Daniel Jones, gives men a chance to tell their side of the relationship story.

CHAPTER 8

Beyond "Opting Out" and the "Mommy Wars"

Out beyond ideas of wrong-doing and right-doing,
there is a field. I'll meet you there.

—RUMI

Figuring out your lifelong relationship to work is another major challenge as you create your life as a Mom. There is no easy solution, no right answer to the life-work equation, but I do encourage each Mom to develop a lifelong view of her career. It can be difficult to take the long view when you are embroiled in the early months of motherhood, but it is a perspective that is worth developing as soon as possible.

Even if a woman decides to stay home until her kids are in school, in many cases that will boil down to a five- to ten-year span. A Mom would have to put forth a creative, concerted effort to reinvent her career at that point, but doing so is definitely possible.

For women who stay committed to their careers, I maintain that it is valuable to keep your options open. As we will see in this chapter, for better or worse, it is essential that each woman is ready to take her career into her own hands if necessary.

Women have such long life expectancies that even after our children have grown, we may have twenty, thirty, even forty productive years of life left to enjoy. Every Mom deserves to nurture her personal sense of self throughout motherhood. After all, when our children grow up and leave home, we will once again be faced with the challenge of reinventing ourselves in a new way and finding our mojo as empty nesters.

✳ Your Life Is Your Start-up

I am drawn to stories of career renewal and reinvention. I feel fortunate to have lived in Silicon Valley throughout my twenties, during the dot-com boom. In the 1990s, it felt like anything was possible. Even though many companies went bust, seeing start-ups take their shots at success demystified the process. Some companies were founded on brilliant ideas, and some were quite idiotic, but this just made me realize that these entrepreneurs were still just people. The atmosphere of innovation was contagious—*everybody else is reinventing their lives; why can't I?* I had been climbing an academic ladder to success my whole life, but I decided to leave the path that was supposed to take me to a prestigious research job in favor of following my passion for teaching. That may not sound like much of a stretch, but when I told my Stanford graduate advisers that I wanted to become a high school teacher, rather than follow in their ivory-tower footsteps, they had to dig deep to muster support for my choice. As far as the university community was concerned, I was now lost to the "leaky pipeline" of women leaving Big Science.

So I had been through the process of changing careers before the complications of marriage and family arose. When I became a mother, it was a welcome stretch to reinvent myself again as a writer. Doing so provided a new outlet for the creative energy that had fueled my teaching mojo. I am quite comfortable for my personal storyline to involve cycles of change and invention. I encourage you to think about the storyline you would like your life to represent. This is particularly important for today's mothers because the storylines recently written *about us* by others have been quite destructive.

The "Mommy Wars" and the "Opt-Out Revolution" have made the media rounds over the past several years. Stories like these may contain grains of truth, but they tend to take on lives of their own as the purported trends outgrow the facts and outlast their usefulness. It is worth examining and debunking these motherhood myths so that we don't give them more power than they deserve. *Ultimately, the challenge to our generation is to write our own storyline about work and family,* and the second half of this chapter will present strategies that will help each of us do just that.

❋ Ending the "Mommy Wars," Once and for All

The media has done its best to fan the flames of the "Mommy Wars" that threaten to divide women into distinct warring camps: stay-at-home mothers versus working mothers. Dr. Phil literally did this in 2003, when he divided his audience into two factions sitting across the aisle from each other, gleefully announced a catfight, and encouraged the women to criticize each other's perceived faults. The complaints about the other type of mother were poorly camouflaged projections of the actual dissatisfactions that each group had about their own lives. This may have made for a shallowly dramatic television segment, but it left every mother watching it feeling both self-righteously angry at other women and defensive about her own life path.

This type of coverage was followed by some highbrow bullying from an older generation of feminists who criticized younger mothers who took a different life path than they did. Linda Hirshman, philosopher and author of *Get to Work:. . . And Get a Life, Before It's Too Late*, comes out swinging at professional women who left careers to stay at home with their children. She claims that doing so is harmful to the individual women, and also sets a bad example for others. "A good life for humans includes the classical standard of using one's capacities for speech and reason in a prudent way, the liberal requirement of having enough autonomy to direct one's own life, and the utilitarian test of doing more good than harm in the world," Hirshman writes. "Measured against these time-tested standards, the expensively educated, upper-class Moms will be leading lesser lives" (Hirshman, "Homeward Bound"). Her fighting words would almost be funny if they weren't so offensive and narrow-minded. I still scratch my head wondering how caring for one's children could be considered "doing more harm than good." Hirshman displays a profound lack of imagination in her judgments, and I would also expect a feminist to demonstrate a greater understanding of the social forces that shape women's decisions about juggling work and family.

Throwing stones from the other side of the aisle, neotraditional writers such as Caitlin Flanagan and Darla Shine sing the praises of domestic life, suggesting that mothers who work are selfish, and that mothers who complain are ungrateful. Darla Shine's book title says it all: *Happy Housewives: I Was a Whining, Miserable, Desperate Housewife—But I Finally Snapped Out of It . . . You Can, Too!*

With enough criticism flying around to dent any mother's confidence, it's no wonder that real-life mothers feel defensive about their own choices and circumstances. No matter what you do, there is always some pundit ready to attack with righteous indignation. Paradoxically, once I realized that arrows are being launched from all sides, I felt some freedom to give up worrying so much about how other people might judge me. There is freedom in giving up a game that is ultimately impossible to win.

The Mommy Wars storyline creates toxic gossip and accomplishes very little. The energy we spend pointing our fingers at other women (while secretly worrying whether we are doing the right thing ourselves) diverts our attention from all that we could be doing to make the world a better place for all mothers. This infighting distracts us from the root cause of most of our problems: an overall lack of respect and support for mothering, and a workforce that has not come to grips with the fact that workers have family responsibilities too. When we criticize other mothers and internally question ourselves, we end up hurting all mothers by strengthening the status quo. As long the focus stays on "What's the matter with Moms?" we will miss the relevant storyline, "What's the matter with the way we treat Moms and families?"

The Mommy Wars storyline writes each of us into a corner, as though motherhood divides women into rigid rather than fluid categories. Thankfully, life is generally a lot more nuanced than that. Your brain doesn't suddenly switch off when you stay at home, and your kids don't automatically turn into delinquents when you go back to work. Motherhood may alter a woman's work-life trajectory in significant and surprising ways, but even an extended break from employment does not mean that she is out of the game forever. Many of us will be in and out of the workforce over time, perhaps reinventing ourselves several times, or starting our own businesses. For those women who stick with their original career paths, juggling work and family is always a challenge, but once they get through those early years, many women find that their jobs get more interesting and that they are rewarded with more autonomy as they rise to senior ranks.

✳ Beyond "Opting Out"

The "Opting Out" storyline proposed that highly educated professional women were happily choosing to leave the work world in droves after having children. Sociologist Pamela Stone started studying this media trend after she noticed that popular stories about women returning home were remarkably similar: "The women love their jobs, they have the greatest employers who accommodate their family responsibilities, but motherhood is the most rewarding job in the world, children are the greatest love affair of their lives, and there is no such thing as quality time and they need to 'be there' for them" (Stone, *Opting Out?* p. 3).

This recurring narrative grew some powerful legs when *The New York Times Magazine* cover story by Lisa Belkin branded it a proactive "opt-out revolution" (October 26, 2003). For those of us who identified with this life situation, this presented an attractive, empowering version of our life stories. We weren't just retreating home like retro housewives; we were actively choosing motherhood. The problem with the idea of this "revolution," however, is that it puts the spotlight on individual women and leaves significant employment issues in the shadows. Moreover, when you look at the numbers, it turns out that opting out refers to a small set of mothers, a statistical blip rather than a fundamental change in mothers' behavior.

Pamela Stone framed her research with the question, "If work had been so great, and their employers so accommodating of their families, why were they leaving?" To answer this, she did something no pundit had done—she did actual sociological research, talking to real women to find out what was going on in their lives. Stone found that rather than joyfully opting out, many women had fought hard to keep their jobs but were pushed out by employers who would not accommodate their real-life, real-family needs. She also documented what she calls the yellow-light effect: Fathers hit the gas and accelerate their careers, while mothers are more likely to hit the brakes. As the male career goes into hyperdrive, the woman feels even more pressure to take on the supportive caregiving role, rather than fighting to continue her own paid profession.

Let's start by taking a look at the potential benefits and challenges associated with two life paths: a flexible career path with a longer break from work, or an ongoing career path, with a mother returning to work after a short maternity leave. This is an oversimplification but it gives us a starting point to appreciate the complexity of integrating caregiving and employment in our current system. In the United States, families are forced to make tough trade-offs between work and family.

Two Life Paths

Flexible Life Path: Time in and out of Employment; Career Adapts to Family Caregiving Needs

Benefits

- A longer recovery period after giving birth is available and breastfeeding is accommodated.
- Parental caregiving for infants and young children is possible.
- Flexible or part-time employment may allow parents to remain employed without hiring substitute care.
- It is easier to absorb changes in schedule, for example, working from home or arranging time off when school-age kids get sick.
- A larger family may benefit.

- More time and energy are available for home-life activities: cooking, holiday planning, gardening.
- More time is available to be involved in activities such as volunteering in the community or serving as classroom parent.
- Parents have the potential to juggle multiple interests.
- Opportunities are available for future career reinvention, going back for additional education, exploring entrepreneurship. You may be able to try something new during a break from full-time employment.

Considerations

- "Mommy track" effects may last a lifetime, on both professional and personal levels.
- If your career is flexible and your spouse's career is not, you will be the one who is expected to bend.
- You may lose touch with your professional identity and up-to-date skills when stepping out of the workforce, and you may find it difficult to get hired after a period of unemployment.
- You need to maintain a sense of power and confidence to negotiate with your partner.
- Family caregiving responsibilities may continue to tip in your direction for years to come, even beyond child rearing. Will family members assume you will provide elder care as well?
- Lower earnings create a significant risk of financial dependence on your spouse. Building a personal financial safety net is an essential priority. At-home parents and flexible or part-time workers may not qualify for insurance and retirement benefits.
- You must develop a lifelong view: Where do you want to be personally and professionally five, ten, fifteen years from now? What do you have to do to reach those milestones? How can you create a pathway to your goals?

What Is Your Plan B If Circumstances Change Tomorrow?
Reexamine this question on a regular basis. As you invest in developing your skills, networking, and a financial safety net, your Plan B options may improve over time.

Continued Career Path: Mom Goes Back to Work Soon After Having a Baby

Benefits
- Higher earning power over a lifetime can lead to financial security and independence.
- Retirement benefits and Social Security credits accrue in your name.
- You have more power to negotiate with your spouse when you are a breadwinner.
- Your commitment to your job strengthens your career's status as an ongoing family priority.
- You potentially gain satisfaction from work and development of professional identity.
- You receive intellectual stimulation and regular interaction with the outside world.
- You have the potential to share child care and family life more equally with your life partner.
- You career track record can lead to promotions and increased job opportunities after your kids are grown.
- If you can make it through the intense years, your job may get easier and more rewarding as you rise to a senior position.

Considerations
- About seven in ten mothers are employed, as a financial necessity or by choice.

- The workplace still operates on an unfair assumption that "ideal workers" have a stay-at-home spouse who takes care of the home front. Working parents may need to endure stressful juggling or hire extra help to cover these duties.
- The "second shift" of work at home can become a problem. Employed Moms still take on more household and child-care responsibilities than Dads. Be prepared to negotiate home responsibilities with your partner on an ongoing basis.
- Quality child care can be costly and difficult to find.
- Even if a salary barely covers child-care costs, the long-term benefits in earnings, job accomplishments, and promotions may make it worth it to push through several challenging years of employment.
- Making the work-family puzzle pieces fit can depend on your employer's willingness to accommodate family needs. You can do all the right things as you climb the ladder and still receive unfair treatment from a boss.
- Moms frequently experience job discrimination ("maternal profiling") or feel pushed out of the workforce even when they want to stay.
- Current laws do not provide adequate protection and support for working parents.
- You should continue to cultivate options that will let you take your career into your own hands if necessary.

What Is Your Plan B If Circumstances Change Tomorrow?
Reexamine this question on a regular basis. Do you have backup strategy if current child-care arrangements, family circumstances, or employment plans change suddenly?

These alternatives are not simply sets of pros and cons that can be tallied up and compared as simple checklists. Any one of these factors can be a necessity or a deal breaker for an individual family, by choice or circumstance. Life throws us many curveballs, and a premature birth, unexpected illness, special-needs child, financial crisis, divorce, or job layoff can mandate a change of plans at any time. So while I talk about life paths, I acknowledge that we do not always get to choose the path that we find ourselves on. We do have the opportunity to try to make the most of our lives and future potential, no matter where we are at this moment, or how far our path may have diverged from our expectations.

Understanding these opportunities and challenges on a deep level gives us empathy for parents whose lives appear to be very different from ours. Loving parents share a bottom line: We care for our families. Motherhood can be an incredible catalyst for activism and awakening our sense of justice. As we experience the challenges of parenting ourselves, we may become inspired to demand better social support for other children as well as our own. Even if my family has health insurance, becoming a mother illuminates the fact that it's absolutely unacceptable that one in eight children in my home state goes without health-care coverage.

Our public policies are out of step with the rest of the world's approach to supporting families. When I attend international conferences, women from other countries express sympathy and outright shock that American mothers get such a raw deal. *Every other industrialized nation in the world* has a national paid maternity-leave policy, often covering a year or more of paid leave, and many European nations offer extensive public child-care options. Some even offer baby-bonus payments or guaranteed income for children. Many American women don't realize how inadequate our policies are in this country until they get pregnant and realize that disability payments may be the only paid leave they are entitled to, if they have elected to sign up for their employer's disability insurance. As each woman tries to put together a maternity leave, she must navigate the unpredictable, often unsympathetic (if not outright discriminatory) maze of human resources at work, and confront the challenge of finding affordable, quality child care.

The details of one family's story can be more powerful than all the statistics in the world. Reading Selena's story in *The Motherhood Manifesto* sealed my commitment to become an activist Mom:

Selena sat down with her husband James to calculate to the hour what kind of maternity leave they could afford for her to take when their second child was born. She carefully planned for two and a half weeks of paid maternity leave, accumulated from unused sick leave and vacation time, plus one and a half weeks of unpaid leave. Beyond that she would have to be back at work at her administrative job at a nonprofit, bringing home a paycheck.

Despite their planning, life dealt the family an unexpected blow when Selena gave birth six weeks prematurely. Baby Connor would need to stay in the hospital for an undetermined length of time, but Selena was sent home the next day. She was faced with an impossible situation: Should she take her time off while he was in the hospital, or wait to take her time off when her baby came home?

Selena made the difficult decision to go back to work so that she could save her time off to care for Connor after he came home. So Selena had her baby on Thursday, was released from the hospital on Friday, and was back at her desk on Monday. She says, "It was the hardest two and a half weeks of my life," as she recalls the ache of being away from her newborn son and the rigorous family schedule she had at that time, getting her older son to and from day care, pumping milk for her newborn, visiting him in the hospital, and working (adapted from Blades and Rowe-Finkbeiner, *The Motherhood Manifesto*, pp. 20–27).

Faced with this reality, when a mother is not even able to take time for her own physical recovery after birth, when even a "sympathetic" employer can't give her what she needs most—paid family leave—isn't it time to declare a truce on petty, largely illusory Mommy Wars once and for all? We have big problems to solve, and so much to gain by working together on issues that affect all families.

FMLA Facts

The Family and Medical Leave Act (FMLA) was signed by President Bill Clinton in 1993 and guarantees up to twelve weeks of unpaid, job-protected leave for any of the following circumstances: the employee's own serious illness, to care for a child, to care for a spouse or parent with a serious medical condition, or to care for a newborn, newly adopted child, or newly placed foster child.

Workers are currently eligible if they:

- Work for a public agency (national, state, local government, public school);
- Work for a private-sector employer with at least fifty or more employees who work at one or more locations in a seventy-five-mile area;
- Have worked a minimum of twelve months for the same employer;
- Have worked a minimum of 1,250 hours in the last twelve months;
- Have a covered medical condition or have a child, spouse, or parent with a covered medical condition;
- Are the parent of an infant or newly adopted child, or are the foster parent of a newly placed child.

By the Numbers

- All public-sector employers are covered by FMLA, and about 60 percent of all private-sector businesses are covered.
- Approximately 80 million workers have taken job-protected leave under the FMLA. The median length of leave is ten days, and 80 percent of leaves are shorter than six weeks.
- Fifty-one percent of covered, eligible workers earn $30,000 to $75,000 per year; in contrast, only 24 percent of covered, eligible workers earn less than $30,000 a year.
- In 2000, 62 percent of employees in covered establishments did not know whether the FMLA applied to them.
- Of the 3.5 million eligible workers who needed but did not take FMLA leave in 2000, eight out of ten reported that they could not afford to take unpaid leave.
- Ninety-four percent of employers say the FMLA has a neutral effect on profitability.

Source: "The Provisions of the Family and Medical Leave Act," National Organization for Women, February 5, 2007, www.Now.org/issues/family/fmla.html.

❋ Reforming a Broken Model of Work

The hard truth is that our current work culture is not set up to support Moms. Mothers may ultimately make different choices, but they often experience the same pressures. Let's take a look at why the current system is broken, what changes are needed to revolutionize work, and what we as individuals can do to take our careers into our own hands while we are waiting for the work world to change.

No woman can compete fairly in a system that operates on the underlying assumption that workers are men who are able to work full-time and overtime, with the support of stay-at-home wives who run the household. Unfortunately, the fact that mothers' lives just don't operate this way makes them suspect employees. Mothers often see their plum work assignments and opportunities for advancement evaporate after they become overtly or subtly "Mommy tracked." Even if a woman just takes six weeks off for maternity leave, the damage may be done as her employer assumes that by having a child, she has made a choice that ends her commitment to her career (Williams, *Unbending Gender,* p. 69).

Other mothers leave the workforce when they can no longer live up to the ideal and are not offered alternative work arrangements that allow them to integrate work and family caregiving. Here again is the crux of the opt-out/pushed-out dynamic. Even childless women may be discriminated against if employers believe that they may become mothers in the future and drop out of the ideal-worker category. Women experience gender as a force field, a powerful, invisible guiding hand that shapes our lives as workers and mothers (Williams, *Unbending Gender,* p. 37).

Even though the current work structure is set up so that women must often choose between work and family, and men can have both, fathers suffer too under this system. Many feel great pressure to be the primary breadwinner, often working in jobs that stretch well beyond forty hours a week. One-third of male workers put in forty-nine hours a week. Ninety percent of men who work fifty-plus hours a week wish they could work less (Williams, *"Opt Out' or Pushed Out?"* p. 34), but even when flexible options are offered, few fathers feel like they can actually take advantage of them because that path is stigmatized as the fast track to a dead end. The typical benefits structure creates another problem: Even if a couple could arrange two jobs that each required twenty-five hours a week each, the family would most likely lose health insurance, which is typically offered only to full-time workers. More substantial options for flexible employment are worth fighting for, and they would benefit both women and men.

The second wave of feminism in the 1970s did a great deal to open opportunities to women who could act as ideal workers, but the right to compete in the male model of work does not address the needs of most mothers. This unfinished business is the great challenge that our generation needs to face head-on. Each of us needs to look at strategies we can use to take our careers into our own hands, even as we work for and wait for systematic change. First, though, we should take a closer look at the challenges of caregiving.

❋ A Revolution of Caregiving

My motto, "Make the invisible work visible, and then divide it fairly," applies to public policy as well as private life. The invisibility of caregiving fuels the myth of the ideal worker. Women and children have suffered under our current system, which still assigns children's care to mothers, and then marginalizes this important work. Gen X and Millennial parents are in a good position to step up as pioneers in a cultural movement to make caregiving count. We have been raised to expect that we would be able to integrate work and family life, and with small children in our lives, we need recognition, support, and genuine job flexibility now in order to make that happen.

I firmly believe that this revolution has a chance to succeed now when it has failed in the past for one very important reason: The Baby Boomers are going to want the same changes that we want. As they head toward retirement, many are not going to be able to afford to drop out of work all at once. They'll want phased retirement, much as young parents might desire significant part-time employment.

The Boomers themselves are starting to see the complex demands of family connections. Even people without children may find themselves faced with daunting caregiving responsibilities as their parents age or become ill. The typical family caregiver is a single working woman in her forties caring for her mother. For others, an ailing spouse or personal health crisis makes it clear that no one can keep up the pace of an ideal worker forever—yet we all still have a lot to contribute to the work world.

The impending wave of elder care will be impossible to ignore for much longer. First, the sheer magnitude of this trend is unprecedented in our society. Seventy-seven million Boomers are racing toward and passing age sixty. The importance and value of family caregiving as opposed to paid care will come into focus as the Social Security and Medicare systems continue to strain at the seams, or even go bankrupt. As we have seen over the years with child care, paid care alone does not satisfy these needs. Families would benefit by having their personal caregiving efforts recognized and counted as a genuine contribution to the social good.

Elder care removes the element of choice from the equation. Mothers have been swept to the side over the years with a hand wave and the idea "You chose to have children, so you choose the consequences—you are on your own." On a societal level, caregiving is *not* a choice. It is a necessity, whether it means caring for elders or raising the next generation. Child rearing is not optional, as all of us will rely on the care and products provided by the next generation of workers. Forming cross-generational coalitions with all people affected by caregiving needs will elevate the status of family needs to an issue that affects all of us, something that is more than "just a Mommy problem" or "just another lifestyle choice." These issues should be framed and discussed in ways that embrace these broad coalitions. As a Gen Xer, I feel like sometimes my generation's needs have been at odds with the Boomers'. Now that we could potentially get on the same side of the caregiving issue, I say let's get on board together. I am more than happy to hitch my wagon to the Boomers' powerful generational engine to work on shared causes.

Finally, as the Boomers do retire, even through phased retirement, there will be a worker shortage to fill their spots. This will give employers more motivation to look at the business case for flexible work arrangements as a competitive advantage, rather than a favor extended to a few workers. Other countries faced with a shortage of young workers, such as Japan, have eventually had to respond by creating a more family-friendly workplace.

Debunking "Work-Life Balance"

As mothers trying to have an integrated life with many facets, we have set our sights on the wrong goal. It's time to debunk "work-life balance." This idea is everywhere and has become a watchword for my generation, Gen X, which has put work-life balance on the map as our highest ideal as we negotiate with our hard-charging Boomer bosses. Although it is usually presented positively, balance is a trap. I argue that balance accurately describes our current unsustainable situation that asks families to do it all . . . on our own. Until we change our thinking on this issue, we are going to be stuck with the same set of unappetizing work-life "choices" that we are faced with now.

Think about it. Who needs balance? Jugglers, tightrope walkers . . . and Moms. The cover of the iconic Mom-lit novel *I Don't*

Know How She Does It shows a woman struggling to balance a briefcase, baby toy, and pacifier. When we tell women to strive for balance, we're really telling them to keep dancing as fast as they can. We are telling them that they are failing to keep it all together without asking for help.

Our balancing act helps hide the unseen caregiving that we provide: unpaid, uncounted, and invisible labor that forms the foundation of family life. If it were counted, women's unpaid household labor would add an estimated one-third to the world's annual economic product, more than $4 trillion.

So if our balancing act is a farce, what should we be aiming for?

Support.

This needs to become our new ideal, our North Star, our guiding metaphor. The motherhood movement should aim for creating a real support network that involves everyone—employers, communities, men, and women. We need a team approach to holding up the world, one that recognizes the contributions that all family caregivers make, a system that does not just expect us to make the pieces fit all by ourselves.

❋ Mojo Power-up for All Moms

The larger social picture is important because any one of us can act only within the larger system, but while we are waiting for the world to change, there are things we can do to bolster our personal mojo. We can strengthen our position for negotiating with a spouse or boss and increase our options. These strategies are beneficial for all Moms:

1. Always invest in yourself. This can include education, skills development, and keeping your creative spark alive. If you are out of the workforce, you can investigate potential future paths and start planting seeds that will bear fruit later. Many entrepreneurs start new businesses on the side while keeping their day jobs. Being an at-home Mom can lend itself to this type of exploration.

2. Investing in yourself includes tending to your self-care and well-being. Learn to ask for what you need from your family, because they are not likely to offer you free time unless you make your needs known. Set high expectations for your family's support and participation. Negotiation experts have found that those who ask for more get more of what they want.

3. Develop financial independence. This can include earning power, savings, and the ability to be satisfied with a less materialistic lifestyle. You need to be actively involved in your family's financial planning. We'll explore these issues further in the next chapter.

4. Include your professional identity in your networking activities. Moms are fantastic natural networkers, but sometimes we forget to include our whole identities. Don't ever be satisfied to be known solely as "Jacob's Mom." Make sure you let people know about your work background and future interests, and ask about theirs. You'd be surprised how many business connections will naturally develop on the playground or in the school parking lot if you broadcast your professional interests. Whether or not you are currently employed, your personal social network may be the source of your next job.

5. If you have an interest, passion, or big dream, find a way to pursue it. None of us will ever find more time, so work with the opportunities you have. Even a few hours of focused attention per week can yield great results over time. I finished a novel and wrote a screenplay by remaining committed to writing while my daughter was in preschool Mondays, Wednesdays, and Fridays from nine to eleven thirty A.M. An evening class once a week can provide a great chance to do something on your own. Signing up for a class creates a commitment mechanism that elevates that time for yourself to a higher priority. These days, most colleges are developing online learning opportunities as well.

6. Build a support network before you need it. I can't emphasize this strongly enough. Ask yourself, *Who's on my speed dial?* How deep is the list of people you could call for help if you had a flat tire or another emergency and couldn't pick your child up from school? Start working on developing these connections. Offer help to your friends when you can, and ask for help and see what kind of response you get. It is crucial to build these relationships before a crisis occurs. What happens if your mother is your sole source of backup child care, and she suddenly gets sick and needs you to take her to the doctor several times a week? Friends, neighbors, family, and community are all key in this situation, and it's so much easier to call on these resources when you need them if you have invested in relationships and developed connections ahead of time.

7. Work when you can. Becoming a working Mom or stay-at-home Mom is not necessarily a permanent decision. I am very much in favor of women working over

their lifetimes, even if they do leave the paid workforce during seasons of caregiving. While many women do follow a career ladder, many others follow a winding path. Women are more likely to be called on than men to alter their plans for any number of life events. Older women have reflected to me that first they raised their kids, then they had a few years of relative freedom before their parents got sick, then a few more years of calm passed, and then their husbands required more of their care. Our lives can feel like cycles of calm punctuated by crisis. I have had to let my own work drop at times in response to various family challenges, which makes me appreciate all the more that if there is something I want to get done, I had better focus on work when the opportunity presents itself.

Until a revolution in caregiving gets under way, within the family and in our larger society, women are still ultimately responsible for making sure that this work gets done. This is the conundrum that I call "life at the intersection of feminism and reality" on my Mojo Mom blog.

You Don't Have to Do It Alone

Networking is such an important activity for Moms. When you meet talented people, it's important to "capture" them into your network, whether that means developing friendships, connecting people into social networks like LinkedIn or Facebook, or getting to know people through traditional business-oriented groups like the Chamber of Commerce.

A couple of years ago I was meeting so many amazing women in my community through my work as Mojo Mom that I decided I needed to find a way to bring them together. It was as though I kept finding dazzling gems on my path, and I wanted to link them together into a necklace. The Mojo Advisory Circle was born, a group of ten women who are either solo entrepreneurs or business partners; we meet at a monthly roundtable to advise one another on life and business. When we started, most of the women did not already know one another, and I did not know all of them well—just enough to know that I wanted to get to know them better. The group has been a fantastic success. The cross-pollination among the members is amazing. After two years of monthly meetings, everybody in the group has participated in a wide variety of professional collaborations with the other members of the group. We exchange ideas in the meetings and create real-world, real-dollar opportunities and results for one another. We have calculated that our networking activities have generated well over $100,000 of added business value for our group members, above and beyond the unquantifiable benefits of investing in both business relationships and friendships.

I feel very fortunate to have met these women and gathered them into an intentional group. We could not have predicted the opportunities that would come along once we created our network, but once we formed the Mojo Advisory Circle, we were able to follow the leads that came from our shared interests.

On MojoMom.com, the fourth session of the free Mojo Mom Party Kit is a guide to forming a Mojo Advisory Circle. Even if you do not create a formal group, you can learn from our experience. When you network with other people, bring your whole self—including your Mom identity—but make sure that you include your professional accomplishments, hopes, and aspirations as well. You never know when the person you meet on the playground or at a classroom meeting could become your next client, boss, or business partner.

🐾 References and Resources

Opting Out? Why Women Really Leave Careers and Head Home by Pamela Stone
  Stone's work is revolutionary because she did actual sociological research, studying the reasons that women left the paid workforce. She communicates her results with refreshing compassion and understanding.

Unbending Gender: Why Family and Work Conflict and What to Do About It by Joan Williams
  Joan Williams's work is a dense read but provides a brilliant legal analysis of gender, work, and family policies.

Kidding Ourselves: Breadwinning, Babies, and Bargaining Power by Rhona Mahony
  Kidding Ourselves traces the decisions that women and men make—usually unwittingly—before and after marriage, and especially after the birth of a child, that lead inevitably to an old-fashioned division of labor at home. She explores game theory and bargaining strategies to help women negotiate a more equitable deal.

The Truth Behind the Mommy Wars: Who Decides What Makes a Good Mother? by Miriam Peskowitz
  Peskowitz was one of the first feminist scholars to take on and debunk the Mommy Wars.

She Wins, You Win: The Most Important Rule Every Businesswoman Needs to Know by Gail Evans
  Forget *Mean Girls*; what we need is to start building a new "old girls' network." Gail Evans fosters win-win scenarios for all women in business.

The Motherhood Manifesto: What America's Moms Want—and What to Do About It by Joan Blades and Kristin Rowe-Finkbeiner

The founders of MomsRising.org explain the challenges that today's parents face, and the family-friendly policies that would improve their lives.

Mothers & More

www.MothersAndMore.org; Local chapters nationwide

Mothers & More is a nonprofit organization dedicated to improving the lives of mothers through support, education, and advocacy. It specializes in supporting "sequencing Moms," who move in and out of the workforce throughout their lives. ·

The Millionth Circle: How to Change Ourselves and the World by Jean Shinoda Bolen

Women of all ages have been forming circles since the dawn of time. Shinoda Bolen explains how to adapt this ancient practice into a transformative force in our modern world.

CHAPTER 9

Securing Your Financial Future

A man is not a financial plan.
—MOTTO OF WIFE.ORG,
THE WOMEN'S INSTITUTE FOR FINANCIAL EDUCATION

A mother's career path may take many forms—a traditional career ladder, a winding path, or something entirely novel. I like the image of a climbing wall—rather than just one path to success, we face a series of choices that may lead us to unexpected places. Whatever path we take, we need to build a personal financial safety net. It is a harsh truth of motherhood that we can't count on employers or benefits like Social Security to be there when we need them. It is up to us to take our financial futures in our own hands. Once we build the resources to weather an unexpected crisis, then we will be empowered to follow our personalized life path with confidence and security.

We all know that having children changes our lives, but the financial consequences of motherhood are often glossed over. Though it's awfully unromantic to think about money when we think about babies, no woman can afford to ignore the financial implications of motherhood. Our conversation about caregiving, relationships, and career reinvention takes place against a backdrop of challenging financial realities. In her landmark book *The Price of Motherhood*, Ann Crittenden examines the economic consequences of motherhood and the social systems that create these consequences:

> *The reduced earnings of mothers are, in effect, a heavy personal tax levied on people who care for children, or for any other dependent family members. This levy, a "mommy tax," is easily greater than $1 million in the case of a college-educated woman. For working class women, there is increasing evidence in the United States and worldwide that mothers' differential responsibility for children, rather than classic sex discrimination, is the most important factor disposing women to poverty. (p. 88)*

Ann Crittenden's own employment history illustrates that our hearts, minds, and wallets are completely intertwined. She took an extended leave from her job at *The New York Times*, a position that paid approximately $50,000 per year:

> *Without quite realizing what I was doing, I took what I thought would be a relatively short break, assuming it would be easy to get back into journalism after a few years, or to earn a decent income from books and other projects. I was wrong. As it turned out, I sacrificed more than half of my expected lifetime earnings. . . . At the time, I never sat down and made these economic calculations. I never even thought about money in connection with motherhood, or if I did, I assumed my husband would provide all we needed. And had I been asked to weigh my son's childhood against ten or fifteen more years at the* Times, *I doubt*

whether the monetary loss would have tipped the scales. But still, this seems like a high price to pay for doing the right thing. (p. 89)

Over a lifetime, the opportunity costs, lost wages, and diminished retirement savings that accompany a break from employment, combined with mothers' exclusion from social safety nets, create a precarious financial situation for many women. Shockingly, *motherhood is the single biggest risk factor for poverty in old age* (Crittenden, *The Price of Motherhood*, p. 6). What we sentimentally refer to as "the most important job in the world" is not only unpaid labor; it is a role that actually creates a lifelong financial burden for mothers.

The facts are clear: As things stand right now, we mothers need to take charge of ensuring our own financial security, even as we work to create a fairer system for all families.

❋ Mothers in the Workforce

The dichotomy between stay-at-home Moms and employed Moms has been overplayed in many ways, but the most important thing that is overlooked is that many women step in and out of the workforce at different periods of their lives, often to care for children or elderly relatives. According to Congressional testimony, while 70 percent of mothers are in the workforce at any given time, on average women spend a total of eleven and a half years out of the paid workforce during their working lives. That still leaves decades of employment for most of us, yet those interruptions come at a cost. Unfortunately, stepping in and out of the workforce can lead to lower earnings and has a negative impact on women's eligibility for pensions. On average, a woman's pension is worth only half of a man's pension—yet women can expect to live seven years longer than men and therefore need to save even more.

Employers need to become more flexible and learn to embrace workers who want to reenter the workforce after "taking time off" to raise children. In an ideal world, paths of reentry forged by parents would help pave the way for all employees to create more livable work schedules and creative career paths. Even independent, "child-free" people may find one day that they need to take advantage of family leave to care for an ailing parent or spouse. We have to ask for what we need, as it is unlikely that these options will be offered to us out of the blue. At the same time, we need to bring these issues to the fore-front of public consciousness, to make sure that pioneering individual change gets translated into policy change in our companies and our public policy. I expect that it will take a generation to fully realize this change, but I believe it will take place, and we are the ones to make it happen.

Whatever our employment choices are, the important thing is to be *conscious* of how our chosen path affects our financial future. *One thing is certain: All of us need a Plan B that we can activate if our best-laid plans get derailed.* This applies to all mothers but has special urgency for women who are not currently earning an income. As much as we hate to even think about it, divorce, widowhood, illness or disability, or unexpected layoffs are potential realities for all families. The stay-at-home Mom arrangement works well for many parents, as long as the couple stays together over the long run, and the primary breadwinner remains employed. However, stepping out of the paid workforce can have disastrous consequences when women find themselves unexpectedly single, or suddenly need to become a major contributor to the family's earnings. This chapter will provide a basic framework for creating your family's financial safety net and will suggest strategies to help you stay competitive in an evolving workforce.

Career Revolutionaries

Focusing on basic financial security doesn't mean that you are a stick-in-the-mud. A nest egg can also give you the flexibility to become an audacious career revolutionary. I admire those people who have unapologetically chosen a different path, or taken the initiative of striking out on their own as entrepreneurs. Here are a few inspiring examples:

Cali Ressler and Jody Thompson reformed the workplace at Best Buy headquarters by creating the Results-Only Work Environment, aka ROWE. Then they set out on their own, creating an independent consulting company to bring ROWE to the rest of the world. When a company adopts ROWE, the culture says good-bye to face time, clock punching, and useless mandatory meetings. All that matters is that you get your work done, and it's literally none of the company's business how or where that takes place, as long as you meet your milestones. ROWE is great for parents and anyone who wants a life. Cali and Jody spell out the details of the ROWE movement in their book *Why Work Sucks and How to Fix It.* I am convinced that a revolution in truly flexible work is coming. Cali and Jody's work will accelerate this process so that change arrives in time to benefit today's Mojo Moms.

Timothy Ferriss is one of the most adventurous lifestyle engineers on the scene. His book *The 4-Hour Workweek* is built on the premise that he wants to create a system that generates an automatic income with little work, freeing him up to race motorcycles in Europe, ski in the Andes, and tango in Buenos Aires. I did not find Ferriss's specific advice to be practically applicable to many mothers' lives, but I love the way that he not only thinks outside the box, but smashes the walls once and for all. His work is a good antidote for those times when other experts try to label Moms as losers for wanting to go off script.

Finally, Kim Lavine tells her story about building a multimillion-dollar company, Green Daisy, around her very simple invention, the Wuvit, a grain-filled pillow that serves as a cozy heating or cooling pad. Kim shares her story in her book *Mommy Millionaire*, which is half memoir, half practical how-to guide to starting your own business. Her writing creates a vivid behind-the-scenes tour of the hard work and guts that go into any start-up company. You need to take risks to reap rewards as an entrepreneur, and Kim is just as honest about the times that she almost lost it all as she is about her successes. She created a job that is incredibly demanding but fulfills her goal of supporting her family financially while spending time with her children. As Boss Mom, she does not have to ask permission or explain herself to anyone when she takes the morning off for her kids' doctor appointments or other family obligations.

Weaving Your Financial Safety Net

While the gender wage gap has been narrowed for women in their twenties and thirties who have never had children, financial vulnerability is an issue for all mothers. The wage gap between mothers and nonmothers is greater than between women and men—and it's actually getting bigger. Women who are not mothers earn 90 cents for every dollar that men make. Mothers make 73 cents, and single mothers make only about 60 cents. *We cannot afford to live in ignorance of our families' financial plans, and the need to construct our own financial safety nets.* I urge you to take the initiative to review your family's financial situation with your partner and a qualified professional adviser. In married couples, too many wives are willing to delegate this responsibility to their husbands. You need access to resources as well as the knowledge and confidence to stick up for yourself. Moreover, in the event of a crisis, you need to know where to find vital financial information. A backup plan is good for the whole family, as it will safeguard *everybody's* financial health and security.

SIX STRANDS OF A MOM'S FINANCIAL SAFETY NET

1. *Solid financial and estate planning.* Make sure *you* understand your family's financial plan, including the location of important documents such as estate planning papers, wills, trusts, stock certificates, insurance policies, real estate closing statements, and college funds. Many documents belong in a safe-deposit box, but some do not. If a box-holder dies, it can be very difficult to access the contents. Consult an attorney or your bank representative to find out the legal guidelines for your state.

   Make sure that your wills are up-to-date, and that you and your partner have designated legal guardians for your children. In a time of crisis, the last thing you want to deal with is a will or financial documents that do not designate the proper beneficiaries.

   Keep phone numbers of estate attorneys, insurance agents, and accountants on file. As you work with accountants, lawyers, and investment advisers, make sure that the experts you hire represent both your husband's and your interests equally. Any advisers you hire should address this issue with you directly, but if they do not, you need to ask them. Most of the time, spousal interests will be in common, but if a particular form of planning benefits one of you at the expense of the other, your experts should alert you of this possibility before the planning is carried out. For example, do your family's wills and trusts protect your interests equally, and adequately provide for your financial needs if your spouse dies first? Unfortunately, I have personally encountered some sexist assumptions in this area, when our lawyers wanted to draw up estate-planning documents that potentially favored my husband at my expense. It wasn't easy to stand up and cry foul, especially since I trust my husband, but I kept speaking up until my questions were answered and a new plan was created that fairly represented both of us.

2. *Build an emergency savings fund.* Do you have an emergency savings fund to tide you over in case of financial need? If not, open a savings account in your name dedicated to that purpose and make fixed monthly deposits to build up your emergency fund. This fund is essential in the face of many different types of emergencies: job loss, partner loss, natural disaster, disability, ill child, or ailing elders. Many families need the equivalent of three to six months' household expenses in their fund, and many experts recommend savings of six to eight months' expenses during a tough job market. You may have to carefully examine your budgetary wants and needs and dispense with some luxuries (cable TV, dining out, entertainment, shopping) while you build up your savings. A dose of frugality is good for all of us, especially as we brace against uncertain economic times. If a breadwin-

ner is laid off, the emergency savings fund can mean the difference between inconvenience and calamity. Savings can also give you a cushion that will increase your bargaining power to hold out for a good job, rather than desperately accepting the first offer that comes along.

It is essential to have emergency savings in an account that is in your name only. If your spouse dies, you do not want to have to get a court order or go through extensive paperwork to recover your jointly held assets. In a time of sudden loss, there is enough emotional turmoil without worrying that you will not be able to access enough money to buy groceries and keep your household running. Your ability to withdraw money from jointly held accounts may be restricted as the estate is submitted to probate, the legal process used to prove the validity of a written will.

In the case of a sudden marital breakup, your spouse could drain funds from joint accounts and leave you with nothing if you do not have savings in your name only.

3. *Use credit, wisely, and develop healthy habits.* Get a credit report for yourself and your spouse to check your family's credit health. Under federal law, you are entitled to receive one free credit report each year from each of the three major companies, TransUnion, Experian, and Equifax. You can request your free report from the Web site set up by these companies, www.AnnualCreditReport.com. Spell the Web address carefully so that you do not mistakenly navigate to a fraudulent site, because you will have to give identifying information to get your free report. Similarly

named imposter Web sites have popped up, and the Federal Trade Commission strongly recommends that you stick with the official site, www.AnnualCredit Report.com.

Your credit score, also known as your FICO score, is a magic number. The FICO scale ranges from 300 to 850: 620 is a benchmark for par, 680 and above is good, and 700 and above is excellent. You want to work your way up to an excellent score by using credit and using it responsibility (Tip #1: Pay all your bills on time). Why? Your FICO score determines not only the interest rate you'll be charged on your credit cards, but also loan eligibility and the interest rate you'll be charged for your mortgage, car loan, and student loans.

For example, the payment for a thirty-year fixed mortgage of $250,000 can cost $700 more per month for a borrower with a poor credit score than for a borrower with an excellent FICO score. That's equivalent to the monthly take-home pay from a decent part-time job! You can see why the FICO score is so important. Experts recommend that you remain patient and raise your credit score to at least 620 before applying for credit, especially long-term credit, in order to borrow at reasonable interest rates.

(Example from Love to Know: Credit Cards, http://CreditCards.LoveToKnow.com/What_is_a_ Good_Credit_Score.)

Each individual needs to develop a solid credit history. Make sure that you have some credit cards and household utilities *in your name* so that paying bills counts toward your positive credit score. If you have credit card debt that you routinely carry over from month to month, develop a disciplined plan to pay the cards off once you have saved half of your emergency fund. When you check your credit card bills and annual credit report, look for suspicious activity as well as mistakes. Many credit card companies offer a credit protection service for less than $10 a month that automatically sends you an alert letter every time a new credit application is filed in your name, as well as detailed quarterly updates of your credit report. This service may be worth the cost for the convenience of automatic notifications when changes occur, as protection against identity theft. Even if you are ultimately cleared of responsibility for fraudulent charges, the hassle is enormous and the damage to your credit history can be difficult to repair.

4. *Review life and disability insurance coverage.* Do you and your partner both have enough coverage? If the primary breadwinner dies or becomes disabled, you need enough money to cover your debts and still provide you with working capital to rebuild your financial plan and support your family. If you are a stay-at-home Mom, is there a life insurance policy and disability policy covering you, so that if you died or became disabled, your spouse could afford to hire someone to do the work you now do for no pay? During a period of low interest rates, you cannot count on a high rate of return on reinvested insurance payouts. As a result, the amount of insurance coverage you need now may be more than you needed a few years ago.

5. *Investigate your parents' financial and long-term-care planning.* Many of us face the real possibility of be-

coming "sandwich generation" caregivers who are responsible for young children and aging parents at the same time. Discussing financial planning with your parents can be stressful, but it is essential to anticipate the needs of parents, stepparents, or in-laws who may require help to stay at home as they age, or plan for a move to a retirement or skilled-care community. Assisted-living or skilled-nursing-care facilities cost thousands of dollars per month. People are living longer with chronic medical problems, so that elders with debilitating conditions may need skilled care for years; therefore, long-term care insurance is a vital safety net for most families. The catch is, elders can qualify for this insurance only by applying for it *before* they need it.

We adult children are therefore charged with the task of convincing our possibly still-healthy parents that they need to get insurance to prepare for the possibility of being incapacitated. Believe me when I say that I understand how hard it can be to discuss this topic. If the thought of having this conversation is uncomfortable, consider the consequences of being caught without a plan: A crisis can bankrupt a family financially and emotionally, and potentially leads to a situation where elders receive less than ideal care. This is yet another situation in which the options are better and crisis is avoided by advance planning. My husband and I have framed this conversation with our own parents by saying that we want to know what they envision for their futures, so that we can help them get the care they want and need, according to their preferences.

It is key to make this a discussion topic for your spouse's parents as well as your own. Whatever their family decides will impact you as well. Even when large family networks exist, the burden of care often falls disproportionately on one family member, usually a woman. *If your parents or in-laws become ill or financially vulnerable, you may end up with the responsibility of becoming their primary caregiver unless other advance arrangements are made.*

6. *Save for your own retirement.* Our generation needs to plan on being self-sustaining at retirement and beyond. Many mothers are surprised to learn that this issue is in some ways an even more important priority than saving for their children's college education. There are more alternative sources for college loans and scholarships than there are to fund your retirement.

   If you retire at sixty-five, and live to be eighty-five, that is twenty years of living expenses and health care to pay for, and it is almost certain that Social Security and Medicare will have to be significantly retooled by the time we retire. One change will be an increasing retirement age, which makes "time off" for child rearing an even smaller season in our overall life spans. It may be typical to work to age seventy and beyond by the time we get there, with creative phased-retirement options offered in a flexible workplace if we play our cards right.

   Our country faces genuine challenges as we move forward. The impending tidal wave of Baby Boomers retiring over the next twenty years will upend the financial models that support our current system of safety nets. The cash-flow pyramid will be turned on its point, as the demographics move toward a society that has more retirees than workers. When I spoke with CPA Bill Bunch about this issue, he pointed out that if we are stressed-out about caring for our parents, our three-year-olds should be absolutely furious, as the inevitable time bomb of generational entitlements will explode when they grow into adults worrying about how to support *us* in our old age. In 2018, Social Security will start paying out more than it collects, and it will exhaust a $2.3 trillion surplus by 2042, the year a person born in 1972 reaches her seventies (*Time*, November 22, 2004). Fiscal responsibility groups such as the Concord Coalition are ringing early warning bells that our current financial budget policies are unsustainable, and we need to change course if we are to protect our children's future.

Unfortunately, neither political party has been willing to address these problems head-on because the issue appears to be political suicide. We need to insist that our leaders address the sustainability of our entire government, so that we can make changes now to ensure the well-being of the next generation. In the meantime, the least we can do for our children is to prepare to support ourselves as much as possible. If these predictions turn out to be too pessimistic and our government finds a way to fix and rescue Social Security and Medicare, then we can all enjoy comfortable retirements on our extra savings, and pass along generous inheritances rather than crushing debts to the next generation.

Building a Nest Egg for the Next Generation

If your family is in a position to contribute to your children's savings *after* funding your own retirement, you can help the next generation avoid the consequences of the "mommy tax." Glenn Ruffenach of *The Wall Street Journal* provides this excellent strategy:

Older women can help daughters and granddaughters jumpstart their retirement plans. An annual contribution of $3,000 to a Roth IRA for just five years—starting when a woman is seventeen years old (assuming she has earned income), and continuing until age twenty-two—should yield a nest egg of $1 million when she hits age sixty-five, thanks to the magic of tax-sheltered compounding (Ruffenach, "Women: Build a Nest Egg," *The Wall Street Journal*, October 3, 2004).

Isn't that amazing? After years of saving for college, $3,000 a year for five years seems like an eminently reasonable amount to invest in our children's futures as they reach adulthood.

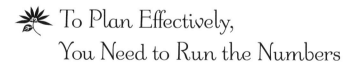 To Plan Effectively, You Need to Run the Numbers

A final word about accounting: CPA Bill Bunch emphasizes the importance of developing accurate budgets to determine our cash-flow needs. You can't know how much money to save in your emergency fund, or how much life insurance you need to buy, unless you know how much your monthly expenses really are. Start keeping track, and keep your accounting as simple as possible. Consolidate accounts as much as you can, and reconcile them manually (with a simple check register) or on the computer. Basic accounting software such as Quicken streamlines these tasks for those who don't mind keeping current with data entry.

Taxes can have a huge impact on your financial calculations. You need to know your marginal tax rate. Your gross salary is not the key number; it is your net take-home pay that will drive your budget. Taxes can impact all sorts of financial decisions—take the example of a person moving from employee status to independent consultant. The individual may have made $40 an hour as an employee, so he estimates that he needs to charge $50 an hour when he becomes a consultant. However, he did not factor in the tax contributions his employer had made, and when all is said and done, he finds that he is really netting much less after taxes than he was as a salaried employee. Consult an accountant, if necessary, to help you factor taxes into any major financial decision or change you are considering.

Money is powerful. We need to get comfortable with the role that this power plays in our lives. Securing your financial future will create a foundation that you can build upon in many ways. You will have more career flexibility and portability if you are not dependent on one source of income, or one job that you cannot afford to leave. If you can save when times are good, and develop an affordable lifestyle, even if you never get rich, you'll achieve a degree of freedom that overextended families can only dream of.

❀ Summary—Two Financial-Planning Checklists

Mojo Mom's Emergency-Planning Checklist

Even worse than thinking about life's possible tragedies is the possibility of being caught by surprise without an emergency plan.

Moms and Dads should both be able to answer yes to the following questions to ensure their family's financial security in case of an emergency arising from unemployment, disability, death, natural disaster, or divorce. Take the time to develop a plan to fill in gaps in your safety net as necessary.

I am familiar with the state of my family's finances and future plans.

I am working to save three to six months' living expenses, held in an accessible FDIC-insured savings or money-market account in my name.

My spouse and I have valid wills that designate guardians for our children.

I have a videotaped inventory of our household's contents.

I can put my hands on copies of important financial records, including bank and brokerage statements, Social Security cards, wills and trusts, and life and disability insurance policies. (Note: In the event of a spouse's death, a copy of the death certificate will be needed in order to access accounts and claim benefits.)

My spouse and I have sufficient life and disability insurance coverage for our family's needs.

I have marketable skills and connections that would help me rejoin the paid workforce to support my family if the need arose.

Mojo Mom's Financial-Planning Checklist

Planning to Start Now

Track your monthly living expenses and work up a budget. You won't know how much to plan for if you don't know how much it costs to maintain your household.

Consider hiring a professional organizer to help you tackle your chaotic filing "system" if you are having trouble getting your documents together. Don't let clutter hold back your future! Professional help will allow you to stop procrastinating and jump-start your financial and estate planning.

Start building up at least three to six months' living expenses in your emergency fund.

Develop a strategy to pay off credit card debt, starting with the card that carries the smallest amount you owe, or the card that charges the highest interest rate. Pay the minimum balances on other cards as you focus your effort on fully paying off one account at a time. Using credit cards responsibly will help you develop a favorable credit history, but make it a discipline to charge only what you can pay in full each month.

Educate yourself about your family's financial plans, and make an appointment to create wills if you don't already have them.

Planning for the Medium to Long Term

Establish your own retirement account, if you don't already have one, and add to it monthly.

Start a college savings plan for your children. State-run 529 plans are a good option to investigate. The 529 plans have investment features similar to mutual funds, and the 529 investment gains are not taxed as long as you spend the money on college-related expenses. You can invest in a 529 plan offered by any state, and you can use the proceeds to pay for college in any state. Some plans can be used to pay for both your own and your children's higher education expenses.

To pay for four years of state college tuition, it is estimated that families need to put away $200 a month from the time a child is born until high school graduation. If you can't afford to save this much, or if your children are nearing college age, work on saving what you can while ensuring your own financial health. Pay down your debts and make sure you are preparing adequately for retirement. College financial aid in the form of grants and loans is an option for your kids. When your children apply for financial aid, your retirement accounts are excluded from the formula used to calculate parental contribution ("A Man Is Not a Plan," *Black Enterprise*, October 2003).

Plan for your possible return to the workforce. Keep your skills and professional licenses current. Consider starting to earn an advanced degree, on a part-time basis if necessary.

Set long-term financial goals for investments and major purchases, such as a home.

Talk to your parents and in-laws about their long-term plans for health care and retirement.

◄ REFERENCES AND RESOURCES

The information in this chapter is intended to stimulate discussion and research. It is, of course, not intended to take the place of professional legal, financial investment, or accounting advice that is tailored to meet the specific needs of your situation.

Thanks to William H. Bunch, CPA, PFS, of William H. Bunch CPA PA and Maze Financial Planning, LLC (www.WilliamHBunchCPA.com and www.MazeFP.com), for his guidance on this chapter.

The Price of Motherhood: Why the Most Important Job in the World Is Still the Least Valued; *If You've Raised Kids, You Can Manage Anything* by Ann Crittenden

The Price of Motherhood provides an eye-opening tally of the costs of child bearing and rearing that fall disproportionately on women's shoulders. Every woman needs to know this information so she can build her own safety net. *If You've Raised Kids, You Can Manage Anything* makes the case that the valuable leadership and organizational skills learned through motherhood are directly transferable to the workplace.

Women's Institute for Financial Education

The Web site www.WIFE.org provides current information about women's financial planning.

Women & Money: Owning the Power to Control Your Destiny by Suze Orman

There are many competent financial experts out there. I like Suze Orman's *Women & Money* because she talks about women's complicated relationships with money, power, and values, in addition to practical investment strategies.

Negotiating Your Salary: How to Make $1000 a Minute by Jack Chapman

This guide will help you during that all-important negotiation and will teach you strategies for reaching the best possible outcome during salary or raise negotiations.

Back on the Career Track: A Guide for Stay-at-Home Moms Who Want to Return to Work by Carol Fishman Cohen and Vivian Steir Rabin

This is a valuable guide for professional women looking to relaunch their careers after taking time away from the workforce.

One Person/Multiple Careers: How "The Slash Effect" Can Work for You by Marci Alboher

Alboher's entertaining guide teaches how to juggle multiple roles and get paid for them.

Why Work Sucks and How to Fix It by Cali Ressler and Jody Thompson

The guidebook for asking for and implementing ROWE, the Results-Only Work Environment.

The Complete Guide to Protecting Your Financial Security When Getting a Divorce by Alan Feigenbaum, CFP, and Heather Linton, CPA, CFP, CVA, CDFA

No one wants to think about or go through a divorce, but all of us will eventually know someone who needs this book. Feigenbaum and Linton provide a comprehensive guide that helps both parties negotiate a fair settlement that takes present and future financial needs into account.

The Survivor Assistance Handbook: A Guide for Financial Transition by Mark R. Colgan, CFP

This slim workbook provides a complete checklist of the things to take care of after a loved one passes away—vital information to help families prepare for and get through a time of transition or crisis.

CHAPTER 10

Spreading Your Wings: Mothers as Leaders

*I read and walked for miles at night along the beach . . .
searching endlessly for someone wonderful who would step out of
the darkness and change my life. It never crossed
my mind that that person could be me.*

—ANNA QUINDLEN

Where has all this talk of mojo led us? This fuel, magic, energy, creative spirit—where will it take us?

That is up to you.

Mojo is power that you can use however you see fit. Mojo is fuel for your enjoyment, your artistic creativity, or your ambitions as a leader. As you generate mojo, I hope that you will experience creative restlessness that makes you feel that you *have to do something*.

The world is facing so many problems that need our attention. Each one of us has gifts, talents, and affinities for different concerns that the world needs us to turn into action. No matter how busy we are, no matter how many children we have, the world simply cannot afford to have us abdicate our positions of leadership for good. Mothering enhances essential leadership qualities including knowledge, organization, and empathy. We become masters of prioritizing. Ask any mother, and she will surely tell you that having children has opened her eyes to what is truly important in life. It is a cruel irony that the same role that gives us so much life experience and wisdom often excludes us from society's organized power structure. As a group, mothers still lack prestige, money, organized recognition, lobbying power, voice, political representation, and job status. To my knowledge, no political party has been accused of being unduly influenced by the special interests of Moms.

Most forms of public debate and leadership are male dominated. Catherine Orenstein of the Op-Ed Project reports that about 85 percent of guests on political talk shows, authors on *The New York Times* nonfiction best-sellers list, Hollywood producers, radio talk show producers, and members of Congress are men. No wonder mothers' concerns are barely represented in public debate.

Every type of leadership has its season, and I am not suggesting that you need to run for Congress while you have young children (though if you want to, go for it!). In the meantime, even when you are busy, you can find an opportunity to raise your voice by writing a letter to the editor of your paper or attending a local meeting on an issue that affects you. No matter where we are in our journey as mothers, we need to remember who we are: powerful, intelligent, creative women. We are leaders within our families and have unlimited potential to become community and world leaders as our time, energy, and interests allow.

Women cannot afford to stay on the sidelines of world issues. Whatever our political orientations are, we need to be aware that our government is enacting key policies and waging wars on our behalf. Our leaders are defining values, freedoms, laws, and priorities with the actions they address or ignore. Do the actions of our government reflect your beliefs and priorities? Your representatives need to hear your support when you agree and your opposition when you don't agree. When you are outraged in silence, you are not accomplishing anything.

Social barriers and internal roadblocks of fear, doubt, complacency, and utter exhaustion keep us from claiming our role as leaders. Our society defines a place for us by paying lip service to the idealized role of mothers, then promptly ignoring us in public discourse. Growing up as girls, then becoming women, and then becoming Moms, we have been taught in ways subtle and overt that if we do anything that makes us stand out too much, we will be pounded down like a nail sticking out of a board. As a result, we've become too good at hiding within the limited boundaries that have been defined for us. A new gap has opened up: the gap between what society expects of us as Moms and the vision and leadership that the world desperately needs from us. Mojo is the energy that gives us a supportive base to ground us as well as wings to raise us to new heights of leadership.

Brave action is needed to close this gap between now-outdated traditional expectations of mothers and the new reality our generation is creating. The fact is, women have more power than they might even realize. Eight-five percent of financial decisions in families are made by mothers—and marketers know it. Think of all of the magazines and advertisements that try to reach women. Think of all of the products we buy for our homes, our families, and ourselves on a regular basis. Buying power is real power, and women should recognize this and use it. As you tap into your mojo, you'll discover and reclaim many sources of power, which will help create the momentum you need to keep moving toward your goals.

❋ Keeping One Eye Open to the World

As busy as we already are, we need to resist the urge to crawl back into our cozy, insulated shells. The path of leadership begins with simple awareness. There is a big difference between being asleep and having one eye open. You may ask, *What can one woman do to address these problems?* My answer to you is that we have the responsibility to open our eyes to problems that affect all of us, and to work actively to make the changes that we can. Instead of being intimidated by potential obstacles, we need to have the courage to ask ourselves, *What is my unique contribution to the world?* and to act on those gifts and abilities.

When you open yourself to the possibility of becoming involved, leadership opportunities will arise. Even an incredibly small first step can eventually lead somewhere interesting. My life changed by watching television—an activity that is theoretically a waste of time. But one day in 2002 I saw Zainab Salbi speaking to Oprah Winfrey, and her message was so compelling that she caught my attention. She had started an organization called Women for Women International (WFWI) that matches American women as sponsor sisters for women who are rebuilding societies recovering from war. Women in countries including Rwanda, Bosnia, Sudan, and Afghanistan are left to pick up the broken threads of civilization and weave them back together again, with few resources and sometimes few rights. The American women provide monthly support and exchange letters with their sisters around the world. WFWI provides job training and human rights and leadership education to their participants.

When I heard about this program, I was so burned-out as a sleep-deprived mother of a toddler that I had just enough energy to get interested. Then I took the small step of becoming a sponsor sister. Later, as I got more interested in WFWI and as I got my mojo back, I wanted to become more involved. I invited Zainab to travel to North Carolina for a weekend series of talks that reached several hundred people. When I started to write as Mojo Mom, I interviewed Zainab about leadership and donated book proceeds to raise money for her cause. By paying attention and taking the small steps that opened up for me, I was able to make a difference in ways that I would never have imagined.

🌿 Becoming a "Naptime Activist"

The Internet has become a vital tool that connects mothers, and in the past few years online action has served as a catalyst that brings women together to not only socialize, but also organize. The motherhood movement has gotten a huge boost from the ability to bring together women to work on common goals, no matter where they live or when they might have a free moment to take action.

Friends and business partners Cooper Munroe and Emily McKhann have walked an interesting path together that beautifully illustrates the Mojo Mom principles of leadership. They are proud "naptime activists," claiming that name to describe women who work on social causes during the limited free time they have. Whether it's naptime, a work break, or before or after hours, the good news is that it is possible to make a difference in just one hour a week. Cooper and Emily have created naptime-activist opportunities for other women through their work in several different venues. Each of their projects has an online component that facilitates one-on-one relationships and action.

Cooper and Emily met in 1988 as coworkers, and they forged a friendship and working relationship that continued to grow after they became mothers. In 2004 the duo collaborated on a book about "parenting in the big picture," and in the process they interviewed people who were looking at the long term and thinking about what they wanted to impart to their own children through their lives. During that time, they also started their Been There blog and became proud members of the mommyblogging community. They were writing about activism and thinking about community building when Hurricane Katrina hit the Gulf Coast on August 29, 2005. They wrote a blog post about how to help rebuild through Habitat for Humanity, but as they watched the catastrophe unfold, they knew they had to do more. "It wasn't enough to just stand there screaming at our television sets," says Cooper. So they took one more step that turned into a giant leap of faith by turning their blog into a "community corkboard" that connected people in need with people who wanted to help. Most of the hurricane survivors didn't have Internet access at that point, but their relatives helped make those connections happen. Overnight, the Been There blog went from hundreds of readers a day to the Been There Clearinghouse, which got tens of thousands of hits. The Internet allowed this decentralized operation to spring to life with a speed that beat FEMA's efforts, and by the Friday after the levees broke, a woman from Chicago had sent down an eighteen-wheel tractor trailer and two vans full of supplies to help families who had evacuated to northern Louisiana.

Notice that their effort was called the Been There *Clearinghouse*, not the Been There *Warehouse*. Cooper and Emily created a catalyst that brought people together. Their effort mobilized many warehouses' worth of goods, but they did so through those one-to-one connections. Mothers who saw suffering reached out to help, knowing that "there but for the grace of God go I." Women who received the lovingly packed parcels, accompanied by heartfelt letters of support, felt that their humanity had been restored. Another person knew and cared about what they, personally, were going through. The psychological impact was as worthwhile as the actual aid they received.

Cooper and Emily experienced profound benefits from their activism. On paper it sounds like their sudden round-the-clock involvement in the Clearinghouse couldn't have come at a worse time, but it turned out to be an amazing blessing. That summer, Cooper had been experiencing extreme burnout with her husband away on business trips, her mother out of town, and four kids, ages one to eight at the time, home at loose ends with few scheduled activities. She hit the bottom, feeling overwhelmed, that it was all too much. But she experienced an enormous mojo power surge once the Clearinghouse opened. I asked her what changed—her sense of purpose or her priorities. She says,

> When Katrina hit, we started to work on the Clearinghouse and we were really making progress, and making these connections, helping people who were actually in really bad situations. It absolutely radically changed my ability to parent. It changed my outlook on life. In a personal way it was very significant to me, and helped being able to handle all the things I have to bear on my shoulders, having four little kids and all the other things that we do in our lives. So it was profoundly personal, as well as all that we were able to accomplish, and I feel that the studies are really right, that the people who are giving back and are actually working on making the world the better place are happier people. They are able to balance more and able to do more. . . . My ability to parent and mother and just being a human being has just been so much easier, bringing this into my life.

This was a turning point for Cooper, the first time she had been a community organizer, and it opened the door for further political involvement.

The Been There Clearinghouse remained active for more than a year, and all the while Cooper and Emily were open to ideas for next steps. Their book idea evolved into a plan to create an online social-networking site for mothers. In the meantime, while attending the 2006 BlogHer conference to talk about the clearinghouse, they met Joan Blades, who was showing her documentary film that accompanied her book *The Motherhood Manifesto.* Cooper learned that a woman named Kiki Peppard was doing work to reform laws in her home state, Pennsylvania, to end job discrimination against mothers. Within days, Cooper had published an Op-Ed piece speaking out against "maternal profiling" in the *Pittsburgh Gazette,* and both she and Emily joined the executive team at MomsRising.org, the online organization that grew from Joan's collaboration with cofounder Kristin Rowe-Finkbeiner.

In the midst of all this, Cooper and Emily kept moving forward with plans to create a new online community for Moms, and they launched TheMotherhood.com in July 2007. They have a deep belief in the Web as a tool for good, the new place to circle the wagons in our incredibly busy, often disjointed lives. It is a place to connect, create, and collaborate. Cooper and Emily want to create a support- ive environment that gives women the extra dose of mojo that they need to get through their daily responsibilities and become involved in causes that extend beyond their families into the world. Emily de- scribes the intentions behind their project:

> *There are an awful lot of women who are just getting by, whether it's finances, or emotional or health issues, or other things going on in their family life. These demands on their time, on their emotions, they're really maxed, between trying to make ends meet and meeting family responsibilities. One of the things that Cooper and I talk about is that hope and dream that if women can support each other in ways that have not been available be- fore, if we can be there for each other to lend a hand, to lend an ear, to offer up resources, that might lighten the load enough so that some women who didn't have time to get involved in things feel like they can.*

Cooper and Emily revel in our interconnectedness, believing that community care and self-care are mutually reinforcing. Community can create the opening that makes awareness and action possible, turning a defensive reaction—"How do you find the time?"—into a belief that each person can find a way to get involved that is personally nourishing as well as beneficial to the world.

❋ Changing the World in One Hour per Week

The Internet is an important new addition to our neighborhood, and a vital organizing tool for busy Moms. By collaborating online you can:

- Reduce isolation by finding your "tribe" and connecting with people who care about the same causes you do.
- Develop friendships or collaborate on projects, freed from geographical and time constraints. Virtual teams can accomplish great things without ever meeting in person.
- Raise your voice through blogging, podcasting, and other forms of public conversation and broadcasting. You can publish an Op-Ed every day on your own blog, or submit your writing to a news and opinion Web site, magazine, or newspaper to reach a wider audience.
- Participate in quick-action alert opportunities to sign on to petitions or send letters to legislators.
- Stay up-to-date and educated about the issues that matter to you most.

Some people say the Internet is impersonal, but to me that's like saying that the telephone is impersonal. It all depends on how you use it. I rely on the Internet to keep me in touch with friends down the street and with people I've known for years, and I have also developed working relationships with friends I haven't met in person yet. Many of my online connections have turned into real-world friendships, but I don't make a hard distinction between the two. This debate could be short-lived, as the next generation grows up being completely comfortable with many forms of communication, from Twitter to Facebook.

In the fall of 2005, Stephanie Wilkinson, editor of *Brain, Child* magazine, wrote an article called "Say You Want a Revolution? Why the Mothers' Revolution Hasn't Happened . . . Yet." She highlighted the difficulty of organizing a diverse, dispersed, and overscheduled network of Moms. Shortly after that, MomsRising.org launched, helping connect mothers within the movement. Less than three years later, MomsRising had grown into an online grassroots movement that involves 150,000 members and eighty-five aligned organizations. What can one Mom do, multiplied by 150,000? MomsRising's grassroots action has helped get paid family leave passed in Washington State and New Jersey. The organization was also instrumental in voicing protest against toxic chemicals in children's toys, and implemented an innovative text-messaging service that allowed gift buyers to look up toys on the spot, to see if they contained toxic compounds. Along the way, individual Moms decorated baby onesies with family-friendly messages to create Power of Onesie displays that have graced state legislatures, the U.S. Capitol, and both the Republican and Democratic National Conventions in 2008.

Seasons of Leadership

Even with naptime-activist opportunities, it may still seem intimidating to look toward leadership outside your family life, when perhaps it takes all the energy you have right now to hold your own clan together on a day-to-day basis. All in due time. When you are in the midst of raising children, small and large, you *are* engaged in essential leadership. At the same time, there is nothing like motherhood to get you to empathize with the challenges that all families face.

Most importantly, I encourage you to *remember who you are*. Don't let your essential self get erased by the daily demands of motherhood. You can be a Mom and a leader. Being a Mojo Mom is all about tending to your creative sparks, ideas, confidence, and ambition. Use every experience. Don't be afraid of what looks like failure. False starts will teach you to recognize success when you see it, and truly, I have seen time and time again that no experience is ever wasted. You may not reach you original goal, but you may have made a valuable connection or learned an important lesson. If you leave one path, take what you have learned with you. Significant life themes will find a way to come around again in another form.

If there is one quality that motherhood demands and teaches, it is patience. As mothers, we plant the seeds of ideas and values all the time, knowing that some of them will sprout and bear fruit, perhaps years later. Some of our most important ideas may be carried on by others in a time and circumstance we cannot even imagine. Zainab Salbi's work with Women for Women International brought her own mother's vision to life in an amazing way when her humanitarian work led her back to her home country in 2003, after a decade of working with women in other countries around the world. She told what it was like to bring her work to Iraq:

> We have three centers in Iraq. The headquarters office in Baghdad is the house my Mom, Suad Al-Wattar, grew up in. The house had been abandoned since 1968, but my Mom would take me there now and then, because it was in front of the river, and if you wanted to go fish you'd go by the house. She'd tell me

stories about how that house used to be when she was a child growing up there. My grandfather was a businessman, and the community by the river was a mixed community of business people and the workers who worked for them. My grandfather was a very generous man who would always have open houses that were the equivalent of a soup kitchen. My Mom would describe these huge pots and spoons they'd use to cook for hundreds of people on these occasions. As a child, I had only seen the house abandoned, and I'd have these imaginations.

Women for Women International organized a community action through which hundreds of women cleaned up the neighborhood. Afterward, a party was held at the headquarters, housed in Zainab's mother's childhood home.

I entered the house, and it was filled with a hundred women in the courtyard. I got goose bumps, because it was exactly my imagination of what my Mom had told me as a child. I was crying as I gave them a welcome speech and as we had a celebratory ceremony. And they all remembered. For me it was a full circle on a very personal level. As a child, I had these images, and now these images are manifesting themselves, through actions I am only doing because I got inspired by my Mom, and what she told me of my Grandfather and my Grandmom's generosity. It was just absolutely amazing for me to go there.

Zainab had literally brought her mother's vision to life. As mothers, as our children's teachers, each of us becomes the world's teacher. We need your inspiration and your wisdom. Find, reclaim, and hold on to the essence that is truly you—creative, powerful, ambitious you. Nurture this aspect of yourself even if it is not yet time to share the full spectrum of your talents with the world.

Nurture your mind. Love it, care for it, allow it to play and roam freely. As we have given birth and tended to our children, let us give the same loving care to ourselves as well.

You have unlimited potential and creativity. I can't wait to see what you do with it.

REFERENCES AND RESOURCES

Necessary Dreams: Ambition in Women's Changing Lives by Anna Fels

Necessary Dreams provides a fascinating analysis of women and ambition, and the social and psychological resistance that prevents women from embracing their ambitious natures. This highly readable analysis lays bare the subtle and not-so-subtle pressures on women to deny their need for recognition and accomplishment.

MomsRising.org

MomsRising.org is a leading online grassroots movement that works to pass family-friendly public policies in the United States.

The Motherhood.com

TheMotherhood.com is Cooper Munroe and Emily McKhann's vibrant, intelligent online community for mothers.

The Mothers Movement Online
www.MothersMovement.org

The Mothers Movement Online, edited by Judith Stadtman Tucker, is another prominent online platform that calls for progress in mothers' organized activism.

The Maternal Is Political: Women Writers at the Intersection of Motherhood and Social Change edited by Shari MacDonald Strong

This anthology includes essays by a variety of mothers who are fighting the good fight, whether in their households or on the House floor.

Family Activism: Empowering Your Community, Beginning with Family and Friends by Roberto Vargas

Vargas argues that the most promising path to change is actually the most accessible and the most universal: the family. In our daily family and friendship circles, we experience countless opportunities to empower, inspire, and support positive change in others. He guides readers to look at those experiences as the seeds of bigger, broader change.

Between Two Worlds: Escape from Tyranny: Growing Up in the Shadow of Saddam by Zainab Salbi

Zainab Salbi's memoir covers her childhood in Iraq, living under Saddam Hussein's regime, her escape to the United States, and the path that led her to start Women for Women International.

The Lifelong Activist: How to Change the World Without Losing Your Way by Hillary Rettig

Rettig's guide to creating a sustainable life and avoiding burnout as an activist is equally applicable to our lives as mothers. She serves up practical management tips that will help managers, activists, and parents alike.

ACKNOWLEDGMENTS

First and foremost, *Mojo Mom* came about because of the inspiring women who helped lift me up as a new mother. To the amazing mothers of Chapel Hill, I am eternally grateful for your friendship, and I am in awe of the example you set.

My family has been with me every step of the way, as a Mom and as an author. Michael has been a loving partner and supportive husband in every way. His steadiness has allowed me to enjoy a winding career path that neither of us could have predicted. And our daughter, of course, made this all possible. She continues to be one of my greatest teachers.

Mojo Mom was written with the input of many women, from informal conversations to lively Mojo Advisory Circle roundtables, as well as MojoMom.com reader questionnaires and interviews with experts and authors. I hope I have captured your spirit along with your voices.

I love the interactivity we have developed online. Over the years, reader feedback from MojoMom.com has kept me going, working hard to learn what's next for Moms.

I am also extremely grateful for the friendships I have developed with other motherhood authors and bloggers. This has been a wonderful benefit of joining the conversation about modern motherhood as it has expanded over the past several years.

This edition of *Mojo Mom* came to life through the editorial guidance of Lauren Marino. Her personal experience and professional expertise were a dynamite combination that shaped the book to make it as widely relevant and current as possible. Lauren's fresh eyes and incisive commentary allowed me to see my writing in a new light, and I am grateful for her attentive investment in my work.

All of this got under way through the effort of Stephanie Kip Rostan, literary agent and Mojo Mom extraordinaire. I will always be grateful to her and the entire team at Levine Greenberg for taking the leap of faith required to make this book a reality.

↘ BIBLIOGRAPHY

Abrams, Melinda, founder of LifePowerCoaching (www.LifePowerCoaching. com). Personal communication, 2004.

Alboher, Marci. *One Person/Multiple Careers: How "The Slash Effect" Can Work for You*. New York: Warner Business Books, 2007.

Aleister Crowley Thoth Tarot Deck. Stamford, CT: U.S. Game Systems, 1972.

Arrien, Angeles. *The Tarot Handbook: Practical Applications of Ancient Visual Symbols*. New York: Penguin Putnam, 1997.

Bahr, Candace, and Ginita Wall. *It's More Than Money—It's Your Life! The New Money Club for Women*. Hoboken, NJ: John Wiley and Sons, 2004.

Barrett, Nina. *I Wish Someone Had Told Me: A Realistic Guide to Early Motherhood*. New York: Simon and Schuster, 1990.

Baskin, Amy, and Heather Fawcett. *More Than a Mom: Living a Full and Balanced Life When Your Child Has Special Needs*. Bethesda, MD: Woodbine House, 2006.

Beck, Martha. *Finding Your Own North Star*. New York: Three Rivers Press, 2001.

Bedore, Bob. *101 Improv Games for Children and Adults*. Alameda, CA: Hunter House, 2004.

Belkin, Lisa. "The Opt-Out Revolution." *The New York Times*, October 26, 2003.

———. "When Mom and Dad Share It All." *The New York Times*, June 15, 2008.

Bennetts, Leslie. *The Feminine Mistake: Are We Giving Up Too Much?* New York: Voice, 2007.

Blades, Joan, and Kristin Rowe-Finkbeiner. *The Motherhood Manifesto: What America's Moms Want—and What to Do About It.* New York: Nation Books, 2006.

Bolen, Jean Shinoda. *The Millionth Circle: How to Change Ourselves and the World.* Berkeley, CA: Conari Press, 1999.

Borba, Michele. *12 Simple Secrets Real Moms Know: Getting Back to Basics and Raising Happy Kids.* San Francisco: Jossey-Bass, 2006.

Bort, Julie, Aviva Pflock, and Devra Renner. *Mommy Guilt: Learn to Worry Less, Focus on What Matters Most, and Raise Happier Kids.* New York: AMACOM, 2005.

Brott, Armin A. *The New Father: A Dad's Guide to the First Year.* New York: Abbeville Press, 1997.

Cameron, Julia. *The Artist's Way: A Spiritual Path to Higher Creativity.* New York: Tarcher Putnam, 2002.

Cameron, Sarah. Personal communication, 2004.

Casarjian, Bethany E., and Diane H. Dillon. *Mommy Mantras: Affirmations and Insights to Keep You from Losing Your Mind.* New York: Broadway Books, 2006.

Chapman, Jack. *Negotiating Your Salary: How to Make $1000 a Minute.* Berkeley, CA: Ten Speed Press, 2006.

Cloud, Henry. *The One-Life Solution: Reclaim Your Personal Life While Achieving Greater Professional Success.* New York: Collins Business, 2008.

Colburn-Smith, Cate, and Andrea Serrette. *The Milk Memos: How Real Moms Learned to Mix Business with Babies—and How You Can, Too.* New York: Jeremy P. Tarcher, 2007.

Colgan, Mark. *The Survivor Assistance Handbook: A Guide for Financial Transition.* 3rd ed. Rochester, NY: Plan Your Legacy LLC, 2006.

Crittenden, Ann. *If You've Raised Kids, You Can Manage Anything.* New York: Gotham Books, 2004.

————. *The Price of Motherhood: Why the Most Important Job in the World Is Still the Least Valued*. New York: Henry Holt, 2001.

Cusk, Rachel. *A Life's Work: On Becoming a Mother*. New York: Picador USA, 2001.

De Becker, Gavin. *The Gift of Fear: Survival Signals That Protect Us from Violence*. New York: Dell Publishing, 1997.

————. *Protecting the Gift: Keeping Children and Teenagers Safe (and Parents Sane)*. New York: Dell Publishing, 1999.

Douglas, Susan J., and Meredith W. Michaels. *The Mommy Myth: The Idealization of Motherhood and How It Has Undermined Women*. New York: Free Press, 2004.

Evans, Carol. *This Is How We Do It: The Working Mothers' Manifesto*. New York: Hudson Street Press, 2006.

Evans, Gail. *She Wins, You Win: The Most Important Rule Every Businesswoman Needs to Know*. New York: Gotham Books, 2003.

Feigenbaum, Alan, and Heather Linton. *The Complete Guide to Protecting Your Financial Security When Getting a Divorce*. New York: McGraw-Hill, 2004.

Fels, Anna. *Necessary Dreams: Ambition in Women's Changing Lives*. New York: Pantheon, 2004.

Ferriss, Timothy. *The 4-Hour Workweek: Escape 9–5, Live Anywhere, and Join the New Rich*. New York: Crown Books, 2007.

Fishman Cohen, Carol, and Vivian Steir Rabin. *Back on the Career Track: A Guide for Stay-at-Home Moms Who Want to Return to Work*. New York: Warner Business Books, 2007.

Flanagan, Caitlin. *To Hell with All That: Loving and Loathing Our Inner Housewife*. New York: Little, Brown and Company, 2006.

Flinders, Carol Lee. *At the Root of This Longing: Reconciling a Spiritual Hunger and a Feminist Thirst*. New York: Harper San Francisco, 1999.

Foley, Sallie, Sally Kope, and Dennis P. Sugure. *Sex Matters for Women: A Complete Guide to Taking Care of Your Sexual Self*. New York: Guilford Press, 2002.

Fox, Faulkner. *Dispatches from a Not-So-Perfect Life: Or, How I Learned to Love the House, the Man, the Child*. New York: Harmony Books, 2003.

Friedan, Betty. *The Feminine Mystique*. New York: Norton, 2001.

Gibran, Kahlil. *The Prophet*. New York: Knopf, 1985.

Gore, Ariel. *The Mother Trip: Hip Mama's Guide to Staying Sane in the Chaos of Motherhood*. Seattle, WA: Seal Press, 2000.

Gottman, John. *Why Marriages Succeed or Fail . . . and How You Can Make Yours Last*. New York: Simon and Schuster, 1994.

Gottman, John, and Nan Silver. *The Seven Principles for Making Marriage Work*. New York: Three Rivers Press, 1999.

Green, Penelope. "Whose Bed Is It, Anyway?" *The New York Times*, March 1, 2007.

Greenspan, Stanley, with Jacqueline Salmon. *The Four-Thirds Solution: Solving the Child-Care Crisis in America*. Cambridge, MA: Perseus Publishing, 2001.

Hanauer, Cathi, ed. *The Bitch in the House: 26 Women Tell the Truth about Sex, Solitude, Work, Motherhood, and Marriage*. New York: William Morrow, 2002.

Harris, Judith. *The Nurture Assumption*. New York: Touchstone, 1999.

Hirshman, Linda. *Get to Work:. . .And Get a Life, Before It's Too Late*. New York: Penguin, 2007.

————. "Homeward Bound," *American Prospect* web-only article, November 21, 2005. www.prospect.org/cs/articles?articleId=10659.

Huber, Cheri. *There Is Nothing Wrong with You*. Murphys, CA: Keep It Simple Books, 1993.

————. *When You're Falling, Dive: Acceptance, Freedom and Possibility*. Murphys, CA: Keep It Simple Books, 2003.

Huber, Cheri, and Melinda Guyol. *Time-Out for Parents: A Guide to Compassionate Parenting*. Mountain View, CA: CompassionWorks, 1994.

Huntley, Becky. *The Sleep Book for Tired Parents: Help for Solving Children's Sleep Problems*. Seattle, WA: Parenting Press, 1991.

Jones, Daniel, ed. *The Bastard on the Couch: 27 Men Try Really Hard to Explain Their Feelings About Love, Loss, Fatherhood, and Freedom*. New York: William Morrow, 2004.

Kadlec, Daniel, Eric Roston, and Jyoti Thottam. "Taking the Plunge." *Time*, November 22, 2004.

Kleiman, Karen R., and Valerie D. Raskin. *This Isn't What I Expected: Overcoming Postpartum Depression.* New York: Bantam Books, 1994.

Lavine, Kim. *Mommy Millionaire: How I Turned My Kitchen Table Idea into a Million Dollars and How You Can, Too!* New York: St. Martin's Griffin, 2008.

Lawler, Jennifer. *Dojo Wisdom for Mothers: 100 Simple Ways to Become a Calmer, Happier, More Loving Parent.* New York: Penguin, 2005.

Louden, Jennifer. *The Woman's Retreat Book.* New York: HarperCollins, 1997.

MacDonald Strong, Shari, ed. *The Maternal Is Political: Women Writers at the Intersection of Motherhood and Social Change.* Berkeley, CA: Seal Press, 2008.

Mackay, Harvey. "Manage Your Time or Others Will Do It for You." www.Mackay.com.

Mahony, Rhona. *Kidding Ourselves: Breadwinning, Babies, and Bargaining Power.* New York: Basic Books, 1995.

"A Man Is Not a Plan." *Black Enterprise*, October 2003.

Martin, Courtney. "'Opting In' to Progressive Parenthood: A Personal Challenge to Modern Mothers." *AlterNet,* May 21, 2008. www.Alternet.org/story/83813/.

Mason, Linda. *The Working Mother's Guide to Life: Strategies, Secrets, and Solutions.* New York: Three Rivers Press, 2002.

Maurine, Camille, and Lorin Roche. *Meditation Secrets for Women: Discovering Your Passion, Pleasure, and Inner Peace.* New York: Harper San Francisco, 2001.

Maushart, Susan. *The Mask of Motherhood: How Becoming a Mother Changes Our Lives and Why We Never Talk About It.* New York: New Press, 1999.

Miller, Karen Maezen. *Momma Zen: Walking the Crooked Path of Motherhood.* Boston: Trumpeter, 2006.

"Mom vs. Mom." *Dr. Phil*, November 10, 2003.

"Mom vs. Mom, Part 2." *Dr. Phil*, September 3, 2004.

"Moms Who Drink Too Much." *Oprah Winfrey Show*, April 17, 2004.

Myers, Gary. *Smart Moms' Babysitting Co-Op Handbook.* Olympia, WA: Tukwila Publishing, 2000.

Napthali, Sarah. *Buddhism for Mothers: A Calm Approach to Caring for Yourself and Your Children*. Crows Nest, NSW, Australia: Allen and Unwin, 2003.

————. *Buddhism for Mothers of Young Children: Becoming a Mindful Parent*. Crows Nest, NSW, Australia: Allen and Unwin, 2008.

Nhat Hanh, Thich. *Peace Is Every Step*. New York: Bantam Books, 1991.

Orman, Suze, *Women & Money: Owning the Power to Control Your Destiny*. New York: Spiegel and Grau, 2007.

Palmer, Parker. *Let Your Life Speak: Listening for the Voice of Vocation*. San Francisco: Jossey-Bass, 2000.

Parker-Pope, Tara. "Gender Roles, Marriage and Anger." Well blog, *The New York Times*, June 10, 2008.

Paul, Marilyn. *It's Hard to Make a Difference When You Can't Find Your Keys: The Seven-Step Path to Becoming Truly Organized*. New York: Penguin Compass, 2003.

Perel, Esther. *Mating in Captivity: Unlocking Erotic Intelligence*. New York: Harper, 2007.

Peskowitz, Miriam. *The Truth Behind the Mommy Wars: Who Decides What Makes a Good Mother?* Emeryville, CA: Seal Press, 2005.

Placksin, Sally. *Mothering the New Mother: Women's Feelings and Needs After Childbirth*. 2nd ed. New York: Newmarket Press, 2000.

Pleshette Murphy, Ann. *The 7 Stages of Motherhood: Making the Most of Your Life as a Mom*. New York: Knopf, 2004.

"The Provisions of the Family and Medical Leave Act." National Organization for Women, February 5, 2007. www.Now.org/issues/family/fmla.html.

Rampersad, Arnold, and David Roessel, eds. *The Collected Poems of Langston Hughes*. New York: Vintage, 1994.

Raskin, Valerie Davis. *Great Sex for Moms: Ten Steps to Nurturing Passion While Raising Kids*. New York: Fireside, 2002.

Real, Terrence. *How Can I Get Through to You? Closing the Intimacy Gap Between Men and Women*. New York: Simon and Schuster, 2002.

————. *I Don't Want to Talk About It: Overcoming the Secret Legacy of Male Depression*. New York: Scribner, 2003.

Ressler, Cali, and Jody Thompson. *Why Work Sucks and How to Fix It*. New York: Portfolio, 2008.

Restak, Richard. *The New Brain: How the Modern Age Is Rewiring Your Mind.* New York: Rodale Books, 2003.

Rettig, Hillary. *The Lifelong Activist: How to Change the World Without Losing Your Way.* New York: Lantern Books, 2006.

Rich, Adrienne. *Of Woman Born: Motherhood as Experience and Institution.* New York: W.W. Norton, 1986.

Rowe-Finkbeiner, Kristin. *The F-Word: Feminism in Jeopardy.* Emeryville, CA: Seal Press, 2004.

Rowinski, Kate, ed. *The Quotable Mom.* Guilford, CT: Lyons Press, 2002.

Ruffenach, Glenn. "Women: Build a Nest Egg." Encore, *The Wall Street Journal*, October 3, 2004.

Salbi, Zainab. Telephone interview with the author, August 26, 2004.

———. *Between Two Worlds: Escape from Tyranny: Growing Up in the Shadow of Saddam.* New York: Gotham Books, 2006.

Schnarch, David. *Resurrecting Sex: Resolving Sexual Problems and Rejuvenating Your Relationship.* New York: HarperCollins, 2002.

Servan-Schreiber, David. "How to Help Your Body Help Itself." *Ode*, November 2008.

Shields, Julie. *How to Avoid the Mommy Trap: A Roadmap for Sharing Parenting and Making It Work.* Herndon, VA: Capital Books, 2002.

Shine, Darla. *Happy Housewives: I Was a Whining, Miserable Desperate Housewife—But I Finally Snapped Out of It . . . You Can, Too!* New York: Regan Books, 2005.

Siegel, Deborah. *Sisterhood, Interrupted: From Radical Women to Grrls Gone Wild.* New York: Palgrave McMillan, 2007.

Spencer, Paula. *Momfidence: An Oreo Never Killed Anybody and Other Secrets of Happier Parenting.* New York: Three Rivers Press, 2006.

Stanton, Melissa. *The Stay-at-Home Mom Survival Guide: Field-Tested Strategies for Staying Smart, Sane, and Connected While Caring for Your Kids.* Berkeley, CA: Seal Press, 2008.

Stone, Pamela. *Opting Out? Why Women Really Quit Careers and Head Home.* Berkeley: University of California Press, 2007.

———. Public lectures given in Durham and Chapel Hill, NC on September 17, 2008.

"Texas Woman Sells Sex Toys, Fights Obscenity Law." May 14, 2004. www. NBC5.com.

Tharp, Twyla. *The Creative Habit—Learn It and Use It for Life.* New York: Simon and Schuster, 2003.

"Top Facts About Women-Owned Businesses." Center for Women's Business Research. May 11, 2007. www.WomensBusinessResearch.org/facts/index.php.

Tucker, Judith Stadtman. "The New Future of Motherhood." The Mothers Movement Online. May 2005. www.MothersMovement.org/features/ mhoodpapers/printpages/new_future.html.

Ueshiba, Morihei. *The Art of Peace.* Trans. John Stevens. Boston: Shambhala, 1992.

Valenti, Jessica. *Full Frontal Feminism: A Young Woman's Guide to Why Feminism Matters.* Emeryville, CA: Seal Press, 2007.

Vargas, Roberto. *Family Activism: Empowering Your Community, Beginning with Family and Friends.* San Francisco: Berrett-Koehler, 2008.

Warner, Judith. *Perfect Madness: Motherhood in the Age of Anxiety.* New York: Riverhead Books, 2005.

"What Is a Good Credit Score?" Love to Know. Love to Know, November 2 2008. http://creditcards.lovetoknow.com/What_is_a_Good_Credit_Score.

"What Mothers Honestly Think About Motherhood." *The Oprah Winfrey Show*, October 8, 2002.

"What Your Mother Never Told You about Motherhood." *The Oprah Winfrey Show*, September 17, 2002.

"What's Hot for Tots Featured Review: BabyPlus Prenatal Education System." What's Hot for Tots, October 24, 2007. www.WhatsHotForTots.com/baby plus.html.

Wilkinson, Stephanie, and Jennifer Niesslein, eds. *Brain, Child: The Magazine for Thinking Mothers.* Lexington, VA: March Press.

Williams, Joan. *Unbending Gender: Why Family and Work Conflict and What to Do About It.* New York: Oxford University Press, 2000.

Williams, Joan, Jessica Manvell, and Stephanie Bornstein. "'Opt Out' or Pushed Out? How the Press Covers Work/Family Conflict." The Center for WorkLife Law, UC Hastings College of the Law, 2006. www.UCHast ings.edu/site_files/WLL/OptOutPushedOut.pdf.

Wilson, Marie C. *Closing the Leadership Gap: Why Women Can and Must Help Run the World*. New York: Viking, 2004.

Winks, Cathy, and Anne Semans. *Sexy Mamas: Keeping Your Sex Life Alive While Raising Kids*. Makawao, HI: Inner Ocean Publishing, 2004.

Wright, Judith. *The Soft Addiction Solution: Break Free of the Seemingly Harmless Habits That Keep You from the Life You Want*. New York: Jeremy P. Tarcher, 2006.

"Woman Fights Arrest for Selling Adult Products." April 29, 2004. www.Click 2Houston.com.

Zander, Rosamund Stone, and Benjamin Zander. *The Art of Possibility: Transforming Professional and Personal Life*. New York: Penguin Books, 2000.

Zoldbrod, Aline P. *Sex Smart: How Your Childhood Shaped Your Sexual Life and What to Do About It*. Oakland, CA: New Harbor Publications, 1998.

INDEX

credit and credit scores, 187–89,
    197
crises, 35, 38–39, 173
criticism, 28. *See also* Mommy Wars
Crittenden, Ann, 180
crying, postpartum, 33
cultural conceptions of motherhood,
    67
Cusk, Rachel, 128

daily activities, 63–64
dancing, 118
danger zone, 111–12, 172. *See also*
    emotions
demands on mothers, 111
depression, 33–34
desensitization, 101, 102
desires, pursuing, 55–57
destructive behaviors, 109–10
development, personal, 145, 172–74
disability insurance, 189
division of labor, 132–35
divorce, 187
dog training, 147
doulas, 27
downtime, 55–56
drama, 116
Dr. Phil (television show), 155
Dr. Spock's Baby and Childcare
    (Spock), 24
drugs, 109–10

educational opportunities, 173
elder care, 169, 181, 189–91
emergency planning checklist,
    195–96

emergency savings funds, 186–87,
    195, 197
emotions
    anger, 107, 111–12, 135, 138–39
    and the danger zone, 111–12
    dealing with negative feelings, 11,
        107–8, 111–12
    and familial patterns, 108–9
    frustration, 107, 111, 141–42
    hopelessness, 33
    importance of expressing, 11
    loneliness, 112
    and marital relationship, 142
    resentment, 81, 107, 135, 139,
        141–42, 145
    and self-destructive behaviors,
        109–10
    vocalization of, 116
    volcanoes metaphor, 110
    See also guilt
employers and employment, 153–77
    and attitudes of bosses, 41–42
    and benefits, 168
    and the broken employment
        model, 166–68
    and child care, 41
    and continued career path,
        161–62
    discrimination in, 162, 180
    and Family and Medical Leave Act
        (FMLA), 39, 165–66
    and family-friendly standards,
        14–17, 41–42, 128, 168–70
    of fathers, 15–16, 159, 167
    flexible work options, 159–61,
        182, 183
    and the four-thirds solution, 131
    and gender roles, 128

About the Author

Amy Tiemann discovered the power of mojo through her own experience of motherhood. She realized that even though her life was heading in a new direction, her prior expertise was valuable and could be applied to a new career as an author and entrepreneur. She applied the research skills she learned earning a Stanford Ph.D. in neuroscience and drew on the creative communication skills she'd acquired as a high school teacher to develop an understanding of mojo that all mothers can embrace.

As Mojo Mom, she has studied the personal transformations of motherhood and the social changes needed to support all families. She works for social action as a member of the executive team of MomsRising.org and as a longtime supporter of Women for Women International.

Today, through her writing, seminars, and Web site MojoMom .com, Amy Tiemann helps other women discover and reclaim a strong sense of self as they grow as mothers and individuals.